Selected
Sonnets, Odes
and
Letters

Crofts Classics

GENERAL EDITOR

Samuel H. Beer, *Harvard University*

PETRARCH

Selected
Sonnets, Odes
and
Letters

EDITED BY

Thomas Goddard Bergin

YALE UNIVERSITY

Harlan Davidson, Inc.
Wheeling, Illinois 60090-6000

Copyright © 1966
Harlan Davidson, Inc.
All rights reserved

Library of Congress Cataloging-in-Publication Data

Petrarca, Francesco, 1304–1374.
    Selected sonnets, odes, and letters.

    (Crofts classics)
    Bibliography p. 137
    I. Bergin, Thomas Goddard, 1904–1987.   II. Title.
PQ4496.E23B4   1985   851´.1   85–20623
ISBN 0-88295-066-5

Manufactured in the United States of America
03 02 01 00 99 15 16 17 18 19 CM

CONTENTS

CONTENTS

Part II: After Laura's Death

CONTENTS

INTRODUCTION

It is difficult to think of any other figure in the history of Western culture who dominated his world of letters as Petrarch did his. By comparison Voltaire, for example, is controversial, Dr. Johnson, for all his fame, parochial. Petrarch's renown was Europe wide, and he enjoyed the respect of the literati and the confidence of princes. E. H. Wilkins affirms that "Petrarch was the most remarkable man of his time; and he is one of the most remarkable men of all time," adding that "he was and is remarkable for his awareness of the entire continent on which the drama of European life was being enacted; for his awareness of the reality of times past and times to come; for the breadth and the variety of his own interests (he was, among many other things, a gardener, a fisherman, and a lutanist); for the high distinction of his writings; for his persistent belief in Rome as the rightful capital of a unified world, governed politically by an Emperor and religiously by a Pope; for his scholarly precocity and for the valiant industry of his old age; for the honors he received and for the hostilities he incurred; for his faithfulness to the study and writing that constituted his most important occupation; and most of all for the vast range, the deep loyalty, and the unfailing helpfulness of his friendships."

Such a summary, despite the list of pastimes and avocations, reveals the "intellectual," as we should call him nowadays, and in fact one may say that Petrarch's life was rather that of a spectator than a participant. He had his opinions and expressed them freely enough albeit discreetly but he did not, as Dante for example did, actually take part in the administration of government, did not, for that matter, ever practice a profession or marry or fight a battle. Of his life he tells us quite a lot himself in his *Letter to Posterity,* which we have included in this volume. The *Letter,* written it would seem no earlier than 1373, breaks off in his forty-seventh year (1351). Instead of

summarizing the poet's own account, we shall add some
supplementary material that he, for one reason or another,
chose to omit. His father, Petracco, a notary of Florence,
was banished in the same year as Dante, but it is not quite
certain whether for like political reasons. Petrarch's mother
was Eletta Canigiani of Ancisa. He had two brothers; one
died in infancy, the other, Gherardo (born 1307) was,
until he entered a Carthusian monastery (in 1342), the
closest friend and confidant of our poet. It was Gherardo
whom Francesco elected to accompany him in the ascent
of Mt. Ventoux (1336). This enterprise, incidentally, has
brought Petrarch much renown as the first man of our era
to climb a mountain "because it is there." Nor does it seri-
ously detract from his glory, though it is very revealing of
his personality, to note that, after reaching the summit and
pausing to take in the view, he opened his pocket volume
of St. Augustine's *Confessions,* and, properly admonished
by the sentence that met his glance, "turned his inward
eye upon himself" and thought no more of the joys of
alpinism.

We may, in general terms, accept the chronology of the
Letter, noting that the years at Bologna were 1320-1326
(with some lengthy absences) and that it was probably
there he came to the attention of the Colonnas, Giacomo,
a Bishop, and his brother Giovanni, a Cardinal, who were
Petrarch's reliable patrons for many years. "The constant
and pure attachment" to which he refers can only mean
his devotion to Laura whom he met, as he tells us in his
sonnets, on April 6, 1327, in the Church of Santa Chiara
at Avignon. This Laura, who is, on the poet's solemn assur-
ance, a real woman, may have been Laurette de Noves,
married to Hugues de Sade. Some readers may find the
embodiment of Petrarch's tender ideal in a matron of the
minor nobility, and one given to frequent pregnancies
(Laurette de Sade had 11 children), not entirely appeal-
ing; fortunately, we are not obliged to accept her candi-
dacy as proven beyond doubt.

Although the *Letter* makes no mention of her, at least
one other woman was of some importance in Petrarch's
life. By her he had two children whom, though born out
of wedlock, he later legitimatized. The elder was a boy,
Giovanni (born 1336), a source of constant vexation to

his father and dead at twenty-four; the other a daughter, Francesca (born 1343), who married the Venetian Bossano and lived to comfort her father's declining years.

The reference to receiving the laurel crown in Rome (Sunday, April 8, 1341), although passed over with modest brevity in the *Letter*, was a precious event in the life of Petrarch who elsewhere tells us that he received on the same day invitations from Paris and Rome, each city eager to bestow this honor upon him. Because he had not really written very much and, in all probability, was not widely known, critics have suspected "the poet's own contrivances" in procuring these flattering invitations. For Morris Bishop the poet's speech on accepting the crown may be thought of as ushering in the Renaissance.

The *Letter* also fails to make mention of Petrarch's enthusiastic encouragement of the "tribune," Cola di Rienzi, who attempted to "restore" the Roman Republic and who appeared for a while to Petrarch as an authentic Roman hero of the past and a likely champion of the political and moral housecleaning so necessary to Rome and Italy alike. The poet's attitude is well expressed in selection liii, which for years was thought to have been addressed to Rienzi.

The *Letter* says nothing of the Great Plague in Italy, which swept away Laura with thousands of others and was perhaps a turning point in Petrarch's life. For at this point, almost eagerly anticipating old age, he began collecting his "trifles," as he called the sonnets, and concurrently collating his *epistolae*, some 500, addressed to friends, contemporary magnates and famous figures of the past and dealing with all kinds of subjects from everyday affairs and encounters to the great themes of virtue, fame and eternal verity.

He wandered restlessly about Italy in the years that were left to him, invited by churchmen, princes and friends to Padua, Milan, back to Vaucluse, and eventually, after a sojourn in Venice, to the little town of Arquà where he died July 18, 1374. Ambassadorial missions had earlier taken him to Prague (1355) and to Paris (1361). But wherever he found himself, he wrote incessantly, composing new works and polishing old ones, releasing them when he thought them sufficiently elegant to circulate. The only work he never circulated was *Africa*, the epic of Scipio's

triumph over Carthage. Although he pinned his surest
hope of fame on this poem, it was one with which he was
never quite content.

Petrarch has been hailed as the father of humanism, be-
cause he handled Latin with a grace unknown in the Mid-
dle Ages and more than that had, unlike his predecessors,
a reverence for antiquity in its own right. He was also a
scholar and a bibliophile—hunter, discoverer and cherisher
of manuscripts. Most of his writings are in Latin: the
epistolae, the minor essays on the "remedies of Fortune,"
"memorable matters," the life of solitude, the wickedness
of doctors and the like. Of especial interest is the intimate
and confessional *Secretum* (Secret). Many of his Latin
verses (see pages 123-131) have about them a pleasant
informal realism that still charms. In Italian he wrote only
the *Trionfi,* a series of visions in *terza rima*—somewhat
reminiscent of Dante but much more medieval in concept
—and the collection of sonnets and odes known as the
Canzoniere (*Songbook*) or *Rime* (*Rhymes*). It is to this
work that he owes his immortality.

The sonnets are not, were not even in their day, espe-
cially "original." The form had been invented a hundred
years before Petrarch made use of it. It is even debatable
how much of the amorous substance is actually "new." It
seems new after the idealizing strain of Dante and his
school, but the Provençal poets in the twelfth century had
in fact expressed the same passionate and wistful dichot-
omies in the presence of the beloved: Bernart de Venta-
dour, for example, sang of his "pure and fine" lady to whom
he offered complete obedience; yet he could also wish for
the "necklace of her arms." Incarnation of earthly beauty
with implications of the heavenly, inspiration of virtue that
is at the same time warmly desirable—if Laura were really
thus, she had had predecessors. The perceptive Coleridge
rightly saw in Petrarch the "final blossom and perfection
of the troubadours." What Petrarch does with this ancient
tradition is to give it unequaled refinement of expression
and, more importantly, bring to the study of sexual love,
with all its paradoxical potentials of joy and anguish, a
deep awareness of the nature of his commitment. Laura,
born to inspire, obsess and also to distract, perhaps even
to mislead, comes close to signifying life itself, lovely but

transient, beguiling, exhilarating but spiritually dangerous. And what is a man to do, when he knows that life is brief though sweet and, being a Christian, knows too that eternity is but a step away? Hence the tenderness, the melancholy, the devotion, the irresolution, the yearning forever destined to be unfulfilled that go to make up the Petrarchan moment of truth, one of such emotional appeal and such psychological validity that, for all its occasional preciousness of expression, it has become a part of the Western psyche. Collecting disciples and imitators through the centuries, this attitude towards love—taken for granted even among those who are unable to tell us when Petrarch lived or what he wrote—is today basic and conventional.

The *Canzoniere* consists of three hundred and sixty-six poems whose order is only loosely chronological, save for the sharp line between poems written during Laura's lifetime and those composed after her death. Very few of the poems can be dated individually with any precision. All we know is that their dates of composition run roughly from 1330 to nearly the end of the poet's life and that he continued polishing and revising into his last years. In addition, he arranged and rearranged these "trifles," which he affected to scorn, on at least three separate occasions.

Not all of the sonnets and odes are likely to appeal to the twentieth-century reader for Petrarch's long and deep influence has been his worst enemy. His songs, so often resung, have perforce lost something of their freshness. A fair number we read today for their historical significance; thus there are in our selections examples of the sonnet of paradoxes, the sonnet catalogue (either sentimental or simply topographical), the sonnet of my Lady's perfection, the sonnet of erudition, the neoplatonizing sonnet and other such categories, all dear to literary historians. One may or may not, after several hundred years of imitators, be moved by them; they are, however, landmarks in the panorama of letters and sentiment. Happily, many more poems, wherein the poet tells us of his love of solitude, his secret crises, his grief and his spiritual conflict, his solace in nature, make us forget the literary pigeonholes. They obliterate the centuries and speak to us in our own language and with our own emotions. Each reader will discover his own. Collectively too, even with all the mannerisms and the now jejune tropes, the *Canzoniere* still has a powerful impact: it is the story, not so much of external events as of psychological experiences on the part of a sensitive, versatile and articulate man. The present selection is sufficiently copious to suggest the significance of the work as a whole.

One may add a word on behalf of the translators represented in these pages. In some ways Petrarch is uniquely difficult to translate for his effect depends not so much on what he has to say as on his manner of saying it. A prose translation of Dante, for example, can be very useful; indeed, it can tell us more clearly than verse the substance of what he says. And Dante is a poet of substance. But a prose translation of Petrarch's sonnets would be a very pallid thing indeed; without something of his elegance, his cadences, his very self-conscious rhymes it would scarcely be Petrarch at all. The translations here presented, for the most part originally chosen for the Limited Editions Club volume of Petrarch's sonnets,* represent the best efforts of skilled and devoted translators. Most of them are of our own century and cast in the idiom of our time, but those by older hands such as Chaucer, Wyatt and Surrey need no apology. Perhaps in defense of both Petrarch and his translators, one limitation, imposed by the nature of the English language, should be pointed out. In Petrarch's original Italian he makes use of hundreds of different rhyming groups; this variety is a calculated element in his approach. In English that many rhymes simply do not exist. This handicap may not trouble us in reading an individual sonnet, but in perusing the collection as a whole one should bear in mind this linguistic fact and accord the translators the proper measure of indulgence. In all other respects the versions included here echo, I believe, very faithfully the style and tone of the original.

* *The Sonnets of Petrarch*, printed for the members of the Limited Editions Club at the Stamperia Valdonega in Verona, 1965

PRINCIPAL DATES IN THE LIFE
OF PETRARCH

❧

1304	July 20th. Born at Arezzo.
1309	Clement V moves papal seat to Avignon. Robert 'the Wise' becomes King of Naples.
1311	Family at Pisa; meets Dante.
1312	Family settles in Carpentras, after journey through Genoa, Marseilles, Avignon. P. begins study of *trivium*.
1313	Death of Henry VII of Luxembourg. Birth of Boccaccio.
1314	Death of Philip IV of France. Battle of Bannockburn.
1316	Begins study of law at Montpellier. John XXII made Pope.
1320	Continues legal studies at Bologna.
1321	Death of Dante.
1324	The *Defensor Pacis* of Marsilius of Padua.
1326	Settles in Avignon following his father's death. Begins ecclesiastical career (he never went further than the minor orders).
1327	6th April, Holy Week. Sees Laura in church of Santa Chiara in Avignon. Edward III crowned King of England.
1328	Lewis IV (of Bavaria) crowned Emperor in Rome. Creates Nicholas IV anti-pope.
1330	In Gascony with Bishop Giacomo Colonna, later returns to Avignon under protection of Cardinal Giovanni Colonna. Composes *Epistolae metricae*.
1333	Travels in France, Germany, Flanders.
1334	Benedict XII becomes Pope.
1336	Climbs Mont Ventoux; travels in Italy (first visit to Rome January 1337; perhaps Spain and England?). Birth of his son Giovanni (mother unknown).

1337   Retires to Vaucluse. Boccaccio writes the *Filostrato*. Beginning of the Hundred Years War. Birth of Froissart. Death of Giotto.

1338   Begins *Africa* and *De Viris Illustribus*.

1340   Birth of Chaucer.

1341   Crowned Poet Laureate by Robert of Naples on Capitoline in Rome.

1342   Takes up Greek. Begins his *Secretum*. Boccaccio writes the *Fiammetta*. Clement VI becomes Pope.

1343   Becomes papal ambassador at Court of Naples. His illegitimate daughter Francesca born. Death of Robert of Naples, succeeded by Joan I.

1344   Begins *Liber Rerum Memorandarum* at Parma.

1345   Escapes from besieged Parma. Attacked by bandits at Reggio. Puts son to school in Verona. Discovers Cicero's letters *Ad Atticum*. Returns to Vaucluse. Local wars in North Italy.

1346   Begins *De Vita Solitaria* and *Bucolicum Carmen*. Clement VI dethrones Lewis IV. Battle of Crécy.

1347   Visits his brother in Charterhouse of Montrieux. Starts for Rome to salute Cola di Rienzi who has made himself master of the city but stops at Genoa on learning of Cola's reverses.

1348   The year of the Plague. Death of Laura. Boccaccio begins the *Decameron*.

1349   Prepares first versions of sonnets, starts to collect his letters.

1350   In Verona, Mantua, Rome, Arezzo. Charles IV imprisons Cola di Rienzi at Prague.

1351   In Padua, where Boccaccio delivers invitation to lecture in Florence. He refuses, returns to Vaucluse. War between Florence and Milan.

1352   Begins the *Triumphs*. Innocent VI becomes Pope.

1353   At court of the Visconti in Milan, where he remains eight years. War between Genoa and Venice.

1354   Boccaccio writes the *Corbaccio*. Final fall of Cola di Rienzi.

1355   Ambassador to Imperial Court at Prague. Writes *Contra Medicum Quendam*. Created Count Palatine. Charles IV crowned Emperor at Rome.

1356   Releases *De Vita Solitaria* and *De Ocio Religiosorum*. Battle of Poitiers.

1357	Releases *Bucolicum Carmen.*
1358	Writes the *Itinerarium Syriacum.*
1361	In Paris on political mission. Returns to Milan to escape plague. Moves to Padua, thence to Venice where he is given a palace by the Senate.
1362	Urban VI made Pope. Langland's *Piers Plowman* (first version).
1364-65	Arranges his letters.
1366	Finishes *De Remediis Utriusque Fortunae.*
1367	*De Sui Ipsius et Multorum Ignorantia.*
1368	Settles at Arquà with daughter and son-in-law.
1369	Chaucer's *Boke of the Duchesse.* Greek Emperor John V visits Pope, Venetians and French, seeking aid against Turks.
1370	Gregory XI becomes Pope.
1372	War renewed between Venice and Genoa.
1374	Possible meeting with Chaucer in Padua. 18th July, Petrarch dies at Arquà.
1375	Death of Boccaccio.
1377	Return of papal court to Rome.

Selected
Sonnets, Odes
and
Letters

LETTER TO POSTERITY

FRANCESCO PETRARCA TO POSTERITY

Greeting.—It is possible that some word of me may have come to you, though even this is doubtful, since an insignificant and obscure name will scarcely penetrate far in either time or space. If, however, you should have heard of me, you may desire to know what manner of man I was, or what was the outcome of my labours, especially those of which some description or, at any rate, the bare titles may have reached you.

To begin with myself, then, the utterances of men concerning me will differ widely, since in passing judgment almost every one is influenced not so much by truth as by preference, and good and evil report alike know no bounds. I was, in truth, a poor mortal like yourself, neither very exalted in my origin, nor, on the other hand, of the most humble birth, but belonging, as Augustus Caesar says of himself, to an ancient family. As to my disposition, I was not naturally perverse or wanting in modesty, however the contagion of evil associations may have corrupted me. My youth was gone before I realised it; I was carried away by the strength of manhood; but a riper age brought me to my senses and taught me by experience the truth I had long before read in books, that youth and pleasure are vanity—nay, that the Author of all ages and times permits us miserable mortals, puffed up with emptiness, thus to wander about, until finally, coming to a tardy consciousness of our sins, we shall learn to know ourselves. In my prime I was blessed with a quick and active body, although not exceptionally strong; and while I do not lay claim to remarkable personal beauty, I was comely enough in my best days. I was possessed of a clear complexion, between light and dark, lively eyes, and for long years a keen vision, which however deserted me, contrary to my hopes, after I reached my sixtieth birthday, and forced me, to my great annoyance, to resort to glasses. Although

1

I had previously enjoyed perfect health, old age brought with it the usual array of discomforts.

My parents were honourable folk, Florentine in their origin, of medium fortune, or, I may as well admit it, in a condition verging upon poverty. They had been expelled from their native city, and consequently I was born in exile, at Arezzo, in the year 1304 of this latter age which begins with Christ's birth, July the twentieth, on a Monday, at dawn. I have always possessed an extreme contempt for wealth; not that riches are not desirable in themselves, but because I hate the anxiety and care which are invariably associated with them. I certainly do not long to be able to give gorgeous banquets. I have, on the contrary, led a happier existence with plain living and ordinary fare than all the followers of Apicius, with their elaborate dainties. So-called "convivia", which are but vulgar bouts, sinning against sobriety and good manners, have always been repugnant to me. I have ever felt that it was irksome and profitless to invite others to such affairs, and not less so to be bidden to them myself. On the other hand, the pleasure of dining with one's friends is so great that nothing has ever given me more delight than their unexpected arrival, nor have I ever willingly sat down to table without a companion. Nothing displeases me more than display, for not only is it bad in itself, and opposed to humility, but it is troublesome and distracting.

I struggled in my younger days with a keen but constant and pure attachment, and would have struggled with it longer had not the sinking flame been extinguished by death—premature and bitter, but salutary. I should be glad to be able to say that I had always been entirely free from irregular desires, but I should lie if I did so. I can, however, conscientiously claim that, although I may have been carried away by the fire of youth or by my ardent temperament, I have always abhorred such sins from the depths of my soul. As I approached the age of forty, while my powers were unimpaired and my passions were still strong, I not only abruptly threw off my bad habits, but even the very recollection of them, as if I had never looked upon a woman. This I mention as among the greatest of my blessings, and I render thanks to God, who freed me, while still sound and vigorous, from a disgusting slavery which had always been hateful to me. But let us turn to other matters.

I have taken pride in others, never in myself, and however insignificant I may have been, I have always been still less important in my own judgment. My anger has very often injured myself, but never others. I have always been most desirous of honourable friendships, and have faithfully cherished them. I make this boast without fear, since I am confident that I speak truly. While I am very prone to take offence, I am equally quick to forget injuries, and have a memory tenacious of benefits. In my familiar associations with kings and princes, and in my friendship with noble personages, my good fortune has been such as to excite envy. But it is the cruel fate of those who are growing old that they can commonly only weep for friends who have passed away. The greatest kings of this age have loved and courted me. They may know why; I certainly do not. With some of them I was on such terms that they seemed in a certain sense my guests rather than I theirs; their lofty position in no way embarrassing me, but, on the contrary, bringing with it many advantages. I fled, however, from many of those to whom I was greatly attached; and such was my innate longing for liberty, that I studiously avoided those whose very name seemed incompatible with the freedom that I loved.

I possessed a well-balanced rather than a keen intellect, one prone to all kinds of good and wholesome study, but especially inclined to moral philosophy and the art of poetry. The latter, indeed, I neglected as time went on, and took delight in sacred literature. Finding in that a hidden sweetness which I had once esteemed but lightly, I came to regard the works of the poets as only amenities. Among the many subjects which interested me, I dwelt especially upon antiquity, for our own age has always repelled me, so that, had it not been for the love of those dear to me, I should have preferred to have been born in any other period than our own. In order to forget my own time, I have constantly striven to place myself in spirit in other ages, and consequently I delighted in history; not that the conflicting statements did not offend me, but when in doubt I accepted what appeared to me most probably, or yielded to the authority of the writer.

My style, as many claimed, was clear and forcible; but to me it seemed weak and obscure. In ordinary conversation with friends, or with those about me. I never gave any thought to my language, and I have always wondered that Augustus Caesar should have taken such pains in this respect. When, however, the subject itself, or the place or listener, seemed to demand it, I gave some attention to style, with what success I cannot pretend to say; let them judge in whose presence I spoke. If only I have lived well, it matters little to me how I talked. Mere elegance of language can produce at best but an empty renown.

My life up to the present has, either through fate or my own choice, fallen into the following divisions. A part only of my first year was spent at Arezzo, where I first saw the light. The six following years were, owing to the recall of my mother from exile, spent upon my father's estate at Ancisa, about fourteen miles above Florence. I passed my eighth year at Pisa, the ninth and following years in Father Gaul, at Avignon, on the left bank of the Rhone, where the Roman Pontiff holds and has long held the Church of Christ in shameful exile. It seemed a few years ago as if Urban V.[1] was on the point of restoring the Church to its ancient seat, but it is clear that nothing is coming of this effort, and, what is to me the worst of all, the Pope seems to have repented him of his good work, for failure came while he was still living. Had he lived but a little longer, he would certainly have learned how I regarded his retreat. My pen was in my hand when he abruptly surrendered at once his exalted office and his life. Unhappy man, who might have died before the altar of Saint Peter and in his own habitation! Had his successors remained in their capital he would have been looked upon as the cause of this benign change, while, had they left Rome, his virtue would have been all the more conspicuous in contrast with their fault.

But such laments are somewhat remote from my subject. On the windy banks of the river Rhone I spent my boyhood, guided by my parents, and then, guided by my own fancies, the whole of my youth. Yet there were long intervals spent elsewhere, for I first passed four years at the little town of Carpentras, somewhat to the east of

[1] **Urban V** died in 1370

Avignon: in these two places I learned as much of grammar, logic, and rhetoric as my age permitted, or rather, as much as it is customary to teach in school: how little that is, dear reader, thou knowest. I then set out for Montpellier to study law, and spent four years there, then three at Bologna. I heard the whole body of the civil law, and would, as many thought, have distinguished myself later, had I but continued my studies. I gave up the subject altogether, however, so soon as it was no longer necessary to consult the wishes of my parents. My reason was that, although the dignity of the law, which is doubtless very great, and especially the numerous references it contains to Roman antiquity, did not fail to delight me, I felt it to be habitually degraded by those who practise it. It went against me painfully to acquire an art which I would not practise dishonestly, and could hardly hope to exercise otherwise. Had I made the latter attempt, my scrupulousness would doubtless have been ascribed to simplicity.

So at the age of two and twenty I returned home. I call my place of exile home, Avignon, where I had been since childhood; for habit has almost the potency of nature itself. I had already begun to be known there, and my friendship was sought by prominent men; wherefore I cannot say. I confess this is now a source of surprise to me, although it seemed natural enough at an age when we are used to regard ourselves as worthy of the highest respect. I was courted first and foremost by that very distinguished and noble family, the Colonnesi, who, at that period, adorned the Roman Curia with their presence. However it might be now, I was at that time certainly quite unworthy of the esteem in which I was held by them. I was especially honoured by the incomparable Giacomo Colonna, then Bishop of Lombez, whose peer I know not whether I have ever seen or ever shall see, and was taken by him to Gascony; there I spent such a divine summer among the foot-hills of the Pyrenees, in happy intercourse with my master and the members of our company, that I can never recall the experience without a sigh of regret.

Returning thence, I passed many years in the house of Giacomo's brother, Cardinal Giovanni Colonna, not as if he were my lord and master, but rather my father, or

better, a most affectionate brother—nay, it was as if I
were in my own home. About this time, a youthful desire
impelled me to visit France and Germany. While I in-
vented certain reasons to satisfy my elders of the pro-
priety of the journey, the real explanation was a great
inclination and longing to see new sights. I first visited
Paris, as I was anxious to discover what was true and
what fabulous in the accounts I had heard of that city.
On my return from this journey I went to Rome, which
I had since my infancy ardently desired to visit. There
I soon came to venerate Stephano, the noble head of the
family of the Colonnesi, like some ancient hero, and was
in turn treated by him in every respect like a son. The
love and good-will of this excellent man toward me re-
mained constant to the end of his life, and lives in me
still, nor will it cease until I myself pass away.

On my return, since I experienced a deep-seated and
innate repugnance to town life, especially in that disgust-
ing city of Avignon which I heartily abhorred, I sought
some means of escape. I fortunately discovered, about
fifteen miles from Avignon, a delightful valley, narrow
and secluded, called Vaucluse, where the Sorgue, the
prince of streams, takes its rise. Captivated by the charms
of the place, I transferred thither myself and my books.
Were I to describe what I did there during many years,
it would prove a long story. Indeed, almost every bit of
writing which I have put forth was either accomplished
or begun, or at least conceived, there, and my under-
takings have been so numerous that they still continue
to vex and weary me. My mind, like my body, is charac-
terised by a certain versatility and readiness, rather than
by strength, so that many tasks that were easy of con-
ception have been given up by reason of the difficulty of
their execution. The character of my surroundings sug-
gested the composition of a sylvan or bucolic song. I also
dedicated a work in two books upon *The Life of Solitude*,
to Philip, now exalted to the Cardinal-bishopric of Sabina.
Although always a great man, he was, at the time of which
I speak, only the humble Bishop of Cavaillon. He is the
only one of my old friends who is still left to me, and he
has always loved and treated me not as a bishop (as
Ambrose did Augustine), but as a brother.

While I was wandering in those mountains upon a

Friday in Holy Week, the strong desire seized me to write an epic in an heroic strain, taking as my theme Scipio Africanus the Great, who had, strange to say, been dear to me from my childhood. But although I began the execution of this project with enthusiasm, I straightway abandoned it, owing to a variety of distractions. The poem was, however, christened *Africa,* from the name of its hero, and, whether from his fortunes or mine, it did not fail to arouse the interest of many before they had seen it.

While leading a leisurely existence in this region, I received, remarkable as it may seem, upon one and the same day, letters both from the Senate at Rome and the Chancellor of the University of Paris, pressing me to appear in Rome and Paris, respectively, to receive the poet's crown of laurel. In my youthful elation I convinced myself that I was quite worthy of this honour; the recognition came from eminent judges, and I accepted their verdict rather than that of my own better judgment. I hesitated for a time which I should give ear to, and sent a letter to Cardinal Giovanni Colonna, of whom I have already spoken, asking his opinion. He was so near that, although I wrote late in the day, I received his reply before the third hour on the morrow. I followed his advice, and recognised the claims of Rome as superior to all others. My acceptance of his counsel is shown by my twofold letter to him on that occasion, which I still keep. I set off accordingly; but although, after the fashion of youth, I was a most indulgent judge of my own work, I still blushed to accept in my own case the verdict even of such men as those who summoned me, despite the fact that they would certainly not have honoured me in this way, had they not believed me worthy.

So I decided, first to visit Naples, and that celebrated king and philosopher, Robert, who was not more distinguished as a ruler than as a man of culture. He was, indeed, the only monarch of our age who was the friend at once of learning and of virtue, and I trusted that he might correct such things as he found to criticise in my work. The way in which he received and welcomed me is a source of astonishment to me now, and, I doubt not, to the reader also, if he happens to know anything of the matter. Having learned the reason of my coming, the King seemed mightily pleased. He was gratified, doubtless, by my youthful faith in him, and felt, perhaps, that he shared in a way the glory of my coronation, since I had chosen him from all others as the only suitable critic. After talking over a great many things, I showed him my *Africa*, which so delighted him that he asked that it might be dedicated to him in consideration of a handsome reward. This was a request that I could not well refuse, nor, indeed, would I have wished to refuse it, had it been in my power. He then fixed a day upon which we could consider the object of my visit. This occupied us from noon until evening, and the time proving too short, on account of the many matters which arose for discussion, we passed the two following days in the same manner. Having thus tested my poor attainments for three days, the King at last pronounced me worthy of the laurel. He offered to bestow that honour upon me at Naples, and urged me to consent to receive it there, but my veneration for Rome prevailed over the insistence of even so great a monarch as Robert. At length, seeing that I was inflexible in my purpose, he sent me on my way accompanied by royal messengers and letters to the Roman Senate, in which he gave enthusiastic expression to his flattering opinion of me. This royal estimate was, indeed, quite in accord with that of many others, and especially with my own, but to-day I cannot approve either his or my own verdict. In his case, affection and the natural partiality to youth were stronger than his devotion to truth.

On arriving at Rome, I continued, in spite of my unworthiness, to rely upon the judgment of so eminent a critic, and, to the great delight of the Romans who were present, I who had been hitherto a simple student received the laurel crown. This occasion is described elsewhere in my letters, both in prose and verse. The laurel, however, in no way increased my wisdom, although it did arouse some jealousy—but this is too long a story to be told here.

On leaving Rome, I went to Parma, and spent some time with the members of the house of Correggio, who, while they were most kind and generous towards me, agreed but ill among themselves. They governed Parma, however, in a way unknown to that city within the mem-

ory of man, and the like of which it will hardly again
enjoy in this present age.

I was conscious of the honour which I had but just
received, and fearful lest it might seem to have been
granted to one unworthy of the distinction; consequently,
as I was walking one day in the mountains, and chanced
to cross the river Enza to a place called Selva Piana, in
the territory of Reggio, struck by the beauty of the spot,
I began to write again upon the Africa, which I had laid
aside. In my enthusiasm, which had seemed quite dead,
I wrote some lines that very day, and some each day
until I returned to Parma. Here I happened upon a quiet
and retired house, which I afterwards bought, and which
still belongs to me. I continued my task with such ardour,
and completed the work in so short a space of time, that
I cannot but marvel now at my despatch. I had already
passed my thirty-fourth year when I returned thence to
the Fountain of the Sorgue, and to my Transalpine soli-
tude. I had made a long stay both in Parma and Verona,
and everywhere I had, I am thankful to say, been treated
with much greater esteem than I merited.

Some time after this, my growing reputation procured
for me the good-will of a most excellent man, Giacomo
the Younger, of Carrara, whose equal I do not know
among the rulers of his time. For years he wearied me
with messengers and letters when I was beyond the
Alps, and with his petitions whenever I happened to be
in Italy, urging me to accept his friendship. At last, al-
though I anticipated little satisfaction from the venture,
I determined to go to him and see what this insistence
on the part of a person so eminent, and at the same time a
stranger to me, might really mean. I appeared, though
tardily, at Padua, where I was received by him of illus-
trious memory, not as a mortal, but as the blessed are
greeted in heaven—with such delight and such unspeak-
able affection and esteem, that I cannot adequately de-
scribe my welcome in words, and must, therefore, be silent.
Among other things, learning that I had led a clerical life
from boyhood, he had me made a canon of Padua, in
order to bind me the closer to himself and his city. In
fine, had his life been spared, I should have found there
an end to all my wanderings. But alas! nothing mortal

is enduring, and there is nothing sweet which does not presently end in bitterness. Scarcely two years was he spared to me, to his country, and to the world. God, who had given him to us, took him again. Without being blinded by my love for him, I feel that neither I, nor his country, nor the world was worthy of him. Although his son, who succeeded him, was in every way a prudent and distinguished man, who, following his father's example, always loved and honoured me, I could not remain after the death of him with whom, by reason especially of the similarity of our ages, I had been much more closely united.

I returned to Gaul, not so much from a desire to see again what I had already beheld a thousand times, as from the hope, common to the afflicted, of coming to terms with my misfortunes by a change of scene. . . .

[*Here the Letter abruptly ends.* The following Epistle, of which we print here only the second half, may fairly be regarded as a supplement. It contains some allusions to events and journeys of the poet's later years and it develops even more fully to self-portrait. The letter is addressed to Boccaccio and dated 1373 from Arquà.]

. . . I certainly will not reject the praise you bestow upon me for having stimulated in many instances, not only in Italy but perhaps beyond its confines also, the pursuit of studies such as ours, which have suffered neglect for so many centuries; I am, indeed, almost the oldest of those among us who are engaged in the cultivation of these subjects. But I cannot accept the conclusion you draw from this, namely, that I should give place to younger minds, and, interrupting the plan of work on which I am engaged, give others an opportunity to write something, if they will, and not seem longer to desire to reserve everything for my own pen. How radically do our opinions differ, although, at bottom, our object is the same! I seem to you to have written everything, or at least a great deal, while to myself I appear to have produced almost nothing.

But let us admit that I have written much, and shall continue to write;—what better means have I of exhorting

those who are following my example to continued per-
severance? Example is often more potent than words. The
aged veteran Camillus,[2] going into battle like a young
man, assuredly aroused more enthusiasm in the younger
warriors than if, after drawing them up in line of battle
and telling them what was to be done, he had left them
and withdrawn to his tent. The fear you appear to har-
bour, that I shall cover the whole field and leave nothing
for others to write, recalls the ridiculous apprehensions
which Alexander of Macedon is reported to have enter-
tained, lest his father, Philip, by conquering the whole
world, should deprive him of any chance of military
renown. Foolish boy! He little realised what wars still
remained for him to fight, if he lived, even though the
Orient were quite subjugated; he had, perhaps, never
heard of Papirius Cursor,[3] or the Marsian generals. Seneca
has, however, delivered us from this anxiety, in a letter
to Lucilius, where he says, "Much still remains to be
done; much will always remain, and even a thousand
years hence no one of our descendants need be denied
the opportunity of adding his something."

You, my friend, by a strange confusion of arguments,
try to dissuade me from continuing my chosen work by
urging, on the one hand, the hopelessness of bringing my
task to completion, and by dwelling, on the other, upon
the glory which I have already acquired. Then, after as-
serting that I have filled the world with my writings, you
ask me if I expect to equal the number of volumes written
by Origen[4] or Augustine. No one, it seems to me, can
hope to equal Augustine. Who, nowadays, could hope to
equal one who, in my judgment, was the greatest in
an age fertile in great minds? As for Origen, you know
that I am wont to value quality rather than quantity,
and I should prefer to have produced a very few irre-
proachable works rather than numberless volumes such
as those of Origen, which are filled with grave and
intolerable errors. It is certainly impossible, as you say,

---

[2] **Camillus** died 305 B.C., defeated the Gauls at Anio at age of 80
[3] **L. Papirius Cursor**, defeated the Samnites 309 B.C.; the Marsi
were a rugged people to the East of Rome; they held their own
with the early Roman Republic   [4] **Origen:** one of the early fa-
thers of the Church, 185?-254?, not always orthodox

for me to equal either of these, although for very different reasons in the two cases. And yet you contradict yourself, for, though your pen invites me to repose, you cite the names of certain active old men,—Socrates, Sophocles, and, among our own people, Cato the Censor,—as if you had some quite different end in view. How many more names you might have recalled, except that one does not consciously argue long against himself! Searching desperately for some excuse for your advice and my weakness, you urge that perhaps their temperaments differed from mine. I readily grant you this, although my constitution has sometimes been pronounced very vigorous by those who claim to be experienced in such matters; still, old age will triumph.

You assert, too, that I have sacrificed a great deal of time in the service of princes. But that you may no longer labour under a delusion in this matter, here is the truth. I have lived nominally with princes; in reality, the princes lived with me. I was present sometimes at their councils, and, very rarely, at their banquets. I should never have submitted to any conditions which would, in any degree, have interfered with my liberty or my studies. When everyone else sought the palace, I hied me to the woods, or spent my time quietly in my room, among my books. To say that I have never lost a day would be false. I have lost many days (please God, not all) through inertia, or sickness, or distress of mind,—evils which no one is so fortunate as to escape entirely. What time I have lost in the service of princes you shall hear, for, like Seneca, I keep an account of my outlays.

First, I was sent to Venice to negotiate a peace between that city and Genoa, which occupied me for an entire winter month.[5] Next I betook myself to the extreme confines of the land of the barbarians,[6] and spent three summer months in arranging for peace in Liguria, with that Roman sovereign who fostered—or I had better say deferred,—the hope of restoring a sadly ruined Empire. Finally, I went to France[7] to carry congratulations to King John on his deliverance from an English prison; here three more winter months were lost. Although during these three journeys I dwelt upon my usual subjects of

[5] in 1353   [6] the mission to Prague 1356   [7] in 1360

thought, nevertheless, since I could neither write down
my ideas nor impress them on my memory, I call those
days lost. It is true that when I reached Italy, on my
return from the last expedition, I dictated a voluminous
letter on the variableness of fortune to a studious old
man, Peter of Poitiers; it arrived too late, however, and
found him dead. Here, then, are seven months lost in the
service of princes; nor is this a trifling sacrifice, I admit,
considering the shortness of life. Would that I need not
fear a greater loss, incurred long ago by the vanity and
frivolous employments of my youth!

You add, further, that possibly the measure of life was
different in olden times from what it is in ours, and that
nowadays we may regard men as old who were then
looked upon as young. But I can only reply to you as I
did recently to a certain lawyer in this university, who,
as I learned, was accustomed to make that same assertion
in his lectures, in order to depreciate the industry of the
ancients, and excuse the sloth of our contemporaries. I
sent by one of his students to warn him against repeating
the statement, unless he wished to be considered an
ignoramus by scholars. For more than two thousand years
there has been no change in the length of human life.
Aristotle lived sixty-three years. Cicero lived the same
length of time; moreover, although he might have been
spared longer had it pleased the heartless and drunken
Antony, he had some time before his death written a
great deal about his unhappy and premature decline, and
had composed a treatise on *Old Age,* for the edification
of himself and a friend. Ennius lived seventy years, Horace
the same time, while Virgil died at fifty-two, a brief life
even for our time. Plato, it is true, lived to be eighty-one;
but this it is said, was looked upon as a prodigy, and
because he had attained the most perfect age the Magi
decided to offer him a sacrifice, as if he were superior to
the rest of mankind. Yet nowadays we frequently see in
our cities those who have reached this age; octogenarians
and nonagenarians are often to be met with, and no one
is surprised, or offers sacrifices to them. If you recall
Varro to me, or Cato,[8] or others who reached their hun-
dredth year, or Gorgias of Leontium[9] who greatly exceeded

[8] **Varro** learned Roman, died 27 B.C.; **Cato:** "The Censor" 237-
142 B.C.   [9] **Gorgias** Greek orator, 485-380 B.C.

that age, I have other modern instances to set off against them. But as the names are obscure I will mention only one, Romualdo of Ravenna, a very noted hermit, who recently reached the age of one hundred and twenty years, in spite of the greatest privations, suffered for the love of Christ, and in the performance of numerous vigils and fasts such as you are now doing all in your power to induce me to refrain from. I have said a good deal about this matter in order that you may neither believe nor assert that, with the exception of the patriarchs, who lived at the beginning of the world, and who, I am convinced, developed no literary activity whatever, any of our predecessors enjoyed greater longevity than ourselves. They could boast of greater activity, not of a longer life, —if, indeed, life without industry deserves to be called life at all, and not a slothful and useless delay.

By a few cautious words, however, you avoid the foregoing criticism, for you admit that it may not be a question of age after all, but that it may perhaps be temperament, or possibly climate, or diet, or some other cause, which precludes me from doing what the others were all able to do. I freely concede this, but I cannot accept the deduction you draw from it, and which you support with laboriously elaborate arguments; for some of your reasons are, in a certain sense, quite opposed to the thesis you would prove. You counsel me to be contented—I quote you literally—with having perhaps equalled Virgil in verse (as you assert) and Cicero in prose. Oh, that you had been induced by the truth, rather than seduced by friendship, in saying this! You add that, in virtue of a *senatus consultum* following the custom of our ancestors, I have received the most glorious of titles, and the rare honour of the Roman laurel. Your conclusion from all this is that, with the happy results of my studies, in which I rival the greatest, and with my labours honoured by the noblest of prizes, I should leave off importuning God and man, and rest content with my fate and the fulfilment of my fondest wishes. Certainly I could make no objection to this if what your affection for me has led you to believe were true, or were even accepted by the rest of the world; I should gladly acquiesce in the opinions of others, for I should always rather trust their judgment than my own. But your view is not shared by others, and least of all by myself, who am convinced that I have rivalled no one, except, perhaps, the common herd, and rather than be like it I should choose to remain entirely unknown.

As for the laurel wreath, it encircled my brow when I was as immature in years and mind as were its leaves. Had I been of riper age I should not have desired it. The aged love what is practical, while impetuous youth longs only for what is dazzling. The laurel brought me no increase of learning or literary power, as you may well imagine, while it destroyed my peace by the infinite jealousy it aroused. I was punished for my youthful audacity and love of empty renown; for from that time wellnigh everyone sharpened his tongue and pen against me. It was necessary to be constantly on the alert with banners flying, ready to repel an attack, now on the left, now on the right; for jealousy had made enemies of my friends. I might narrate in this connection many occurrences which would fill you with astonishment. In a word, the laurel made me known only to be tormented; without it, I should have led that best of all lives, as many deem, a life of obscurity and peace.

You put the finishing touch to your argument, it seems to me, when you urge me to do all that I can to prolong my life as a joy to my friends, and first and foremost as a solace to you in your declining years, because, as you say, you desire when you depart hence to leave me still alive. Alas! our friend Simonides[10] also expressed this wish —a wish but too speedily granted: if there were any order in human affairs, it is he who should have survived me. My own desires are, however, directly opposed to those which my friends—you in particular—harbour, I should prefer to die while you are all still alive, and leave those behind in whose memory and conversation I should still live, who would aid me by their prayers, and by whom I should continue to be loved and cherished. Except a pure conscience, I believe there is no solace so grateful to the dying as this.

If your counsels spring from the belief that I cling tenaciously to life, you are entirely mistaken. Why should I

[10] **Simonides** name by which Petrarch addressed his friend Francesco Nelli (died 1363) to whom he dedicated his *Letters of Old Age*

wish to prolong my existence among customs and manners
which make me constantly deplore that I have fallen on
such times? To omit more serious disorders, I am afflicted
by the perverted and indecent clothing of a most frivolous
set of men. I have already too often complained of them,
both in speech and writing, but words are powerless to
quiet my indignation and distress of mind. These fellows,
who called themselves Italians, and were, indeed, born in
Italy, do all they can to appear like barbarians. Would that
they were barbarians, that my eyes and those of the true
Italians might be delivered from so shameful a spectacle!
May God Omnipotent confound them, living and dead!
Not satisfied with sacrificing by their pusillanimity the
virtues of our ancestors, the glory of war, and all the arts
of peace, they dishonour in their frenzy the speech and
dress of our country, so that we may consider our fore-
fathers happy to have passed away in good time, and may
envy even the blind, who are spared the sight of these
things.

Finally, you ask me to pardon you for venturing to
advise me and for prescribing a mode of life, namely,
that I hereafter abstain from mental exertion and from
my customary labours and vigils, and endeavour to restore,
by complete rest and sleep, the ravages wrought by ad-
vancing years and prolonged study. I will not pardon you,
but I thank you, well aware of the affection which makes
you a physician for me, although you refuse to be one for
yourself. I beg, however, that you will obey me, although
I refuse to obey you, and will let me persuade you that,
even if I were most tenacious of life, which I am not, I
should assuredly only die the sooner if I followed your
advice. Continued work and application form my soul's
nourishment. So soon as I commenced to rest and relax
I should cease to live. I know my own powers. I am not
fitted for other kinds of work, but my reading and writing,
which you would have me discontinue, are easy tasks,
nay, they are a delightful rest, and relieve the burden of
heavier anxieties. There is no lighter burden, nor more
agreeable, than a pen. Other pleasures fail us, or wound
us while they charm; but the pen we take up rejoicing
and lay down with satisfaction, for it has the power to
advantage not only its lord and master, but many others
as well, even though they be far away,—sometimes, in-

deed, though they be not born for thousands of years to come. I believe that I speak but the strict truth when I claim that as there is none among earthly delights more noble than literature, so there is none so lasting, none gentler, or more faithful; there is none which accompanies its possessor through the vicissitudes of life at so small a cost of effort or anxiety.

Pardon me then, my brother, pardon me. I am disposed to believe anything that you say, but I cannot accept your opinion in this matter. However you may describe me (and nothing is impossible to the pen of a learned and eloquent writer), I must still endeavour, if I am a nullity, to become something; if already of some account, to become a little more worthy; and if I were really great, which I am not, I should strive, so far as in me lay, to become greater, even the greatest. May I not be allowed to appropriate the magnificent reply of that fierce barbarian who, when urged to spare himself continued exertions, since he already enjoyed sufficient renown, responded, "The greater I am, the greater shall be my efforts"? Words worthy of another than a barbarian! They are graven on my heart, and the letter which follows this will show you how far I am from following your exhortations to idleness. Not satisfied with gigantic enterprises, for which this brief life of ours does not suffice, and would not if doubled in length, I am always on the alert for new and uncalled-for undertakings,—so distasteful to me is sleep and dreary repose. Do you not know that passage from Ecclesiasticus, "When man has finished his researches, he is but at the beginning, and when he rests, then doth he labour"? I seem to myself to have but begun; whatever you and others may think, this is my verdict. If in the meanwhile the end, which certainly cannot be far off, should come, I would that it might find me still young. But as I cannot, in the nature of things, hope for that, I desire that death find me reading and writing, or, if it please Christ, praying and in tears.

Farewell, and remember me. May you be happy and persevere manfully.

FROM THE CANZONIERE

Part I: Laura Living

I: Sonnet 1 *

O ye who in these scattered rhymes may hear
The echoes of the sighs that fed my heart
In errant youth, for I was then, in part
Another man from what I now appear,
If you have learned by proof how Love can sear,   5
Then for these varied verses where I chart
Its vain and empty hope and vainer smart
Pardon I may beseech, nay, Pity's tear.
For now I see how once my story spread
And I became a wonder to mankind   10
So in my heart I feel ashamed—alas,
That nought but shame my vanities have bred,
And penance, and the knowledge of clear mind
That earthly joys are dreams that swiftly pass.

* Placed first but obviously written late. It was clearly meant to
serve as an introduction to an "edition." Perhaps 1348-9, less
likely 1356-9

II: Sonnet 2 *

Determined with one sally to erase
The memory of countless slights, intent
On winsome vengeance. Love the cheater bent
His hidden bow and chose well time and place.
5 Within my heart's protective carapace
My spirit tarried, ready to resent
Aggression, had my eyes their message sent,
But the swift onslaught gave no breathing space.
Ah luckless garrison, that could repel
10 All earlier sieges, taken by surprise
In this assault what could you do but yield?
No weapon served, no inner citadel
Either to offer war or temporize—
My shattered soul, what feeble arms we wield!

III: Sonnet 3

It was the day the sun had overcast,
In pity of his Maker, his bright sheen
When I fell prey to peril unforeseen,
For your eyes, lady, caught and held me fast.
5 I took no care to shelter 'gainst Love's blast
Wherefore, amidst the melancholy scene
Of dole and penance, my own anguish keen
Was born that has the general grief surpassed.
Through eyes that now but serve to weep my ills
10 Love stormed my heart as I walked unalarmed,
Thinking that day I might pay him no heed.
Meanwhile to you, secure and fully armed,
He did not even show his shaft that kills—
Here's shabby glory for great Love, indeed!

* Perhaps 1327

[1] **the day** Good Friday, April 10, 1327; elsewhere the date of
enamorment is given as April 6

IV: Sonnet 4

He who with foresight boundless and divine
Showed in His office proof of wondrous art,
Who shaped our globe, its each and every part,
Formed fearsome Mars and made a Jove benign;
Coming on earth, His promise to define,   5
Which ancient prophets darkly did impart,
Called Peter, caused John from his nets to part,
And set them in His heaven crystalline.
A-borning He shed not on Rome His grace
But on poor Judah, for His purpose high   10
Is e'er to raise the lowly of this earth.
Whence such a sun shines on our humble place
As to call blessings on its happy sky
Whereunder my fair lady came to birth.

V: Sonnet 5 *

When, you to call, I rouse these sighs of mine,
And speak the name, which in my heart I wear
Love-chiselled, then to spread a sound in air,
Like LAUd, the first sweet elements combine.
Your REgal nature, which the next define,   5
Doubleth my courage for this feat so rare;
But "TArry," cries the last; "for honours there
To carry, needeth stouter backs than thine."
And thus to LAUd you and REvere the name
And the sound teach me, whencesoe'er they come;   10
Yours all our praise and reverence must be—
Unless Dan Phoebus it may haply shame,
That mortal tongue should saucily presume
To noise his green-ever-abiding tree.

[12] **humble place** possibly the hill of Picabré, above Caumont

* Another early sonnet (1328-9); **Laura** was probably known
as **Laureta**

VII: Sonnet 7 *

Sloth, gluttony, and lazy lassitude
Have from the world stolen all virtue away;
Hence from its rightful course has gone astray
Our nature, bound in chains by habitude;
5 And so far spent is every kindly ray
Of heaven that gives us its beatitude
That he is held with madness nigh endued,
Who by the Muses' fountain longs to stray.
Who wishes laurel? Who myrtle on his brow?
10 "In rags and naked, go, philosophy!"
Says the vile crowd, intent on thoughts of gain.
Few comrades will you have to cheer you now.
Therefore, I pray you the more fervently,
Lay not aside your noble task as vain.

XII: Sonnet 11

If it be destined that my life, from thine
Divided, yet with thine shall linger on
Till, in the later twilight of Decline,
I may behold those Eyes, their lustre gone;
5 When the gold tresses that enrich thy brow
Shall all be faded into silver-gray,
From which the wreaths that well bedeck them now
For many a Summer shall have fall'n away:
Then should I dare to whisper in your ears
10 The pent-up Passion of so long ago,
That Love which hath survived the wreck of years
Hath little else to pray for, or bestow,
Thou wilt not to the broken heart deny
The boon of one too-late relenting sigh.

* It is not certain to whom this sonnet is addressed

XV: Sonnet 13 *

Backward at every weary step and slow
These limbs I turn which with great pain I bear;
Then take I comfort from the fragrant air
That breathes from thee, and sighing onward go.
But when I think how joy is turned to woe,   5
Remembering my short life and whence I fare,
I stay my feet for anguish and despair,
And cast my tearful eyes on earth below.
At times amid the storm of misery
This doubt assails me: how frail limbs and poor   10
Can severed from their spirit hope to live.
Then answers Love: Hast thou no memory
How I to lovers this great guerdon give,
Free from all human bondage to endure?

XVI: Sonnet 14

The ancient greybeard shoulders on his load
And quits the home of all his many days
Under the silent loving-fearful gaze
Of eyes forfending what the hearts forebode.
Thence in life's end his old ambitions goad   5
His quaking shanks into long longed-for ways:
Only the burning of his will upstays
Him, by years broken, spent by the long road.
But so at last his yearning brings him nigh
To Rome, to look upon the painted face   10
Of Him whom soon in heaven he hopes to view;
Ah, Donna, Donna, even so go I,
Seeking forever in whatever place
Some crudely-copied shadowy hint of you.

* Perhaps on the occasion of the trip to Rome 1336-7, as apparently also Sonnet 14 [10-11] the veronica, or towel said to preserve the imprint of Christ's face, kept in the Vatican

XIX: Sonnet 17

Some fowles there be, that haue so perfit sight
Against the sunne their eies for to defend:
And some, because the light doth them offend,
Neuer appeare, but in the darke, or night.
5 Other reioyce, to se the fire so bryght,
And wene to play in it, as they pretend:
But find contrary of it, that they intend.
Alas, of that sort may I be, by right.
For to withstand her loke I am not able:
10 Yet can I not hide me in no dark place:
So foloweth me remembrance of that face:
That with my teary eyn, swolne, and vnstable,
My desteny to beholde her doth me lead:
And yet I knowe, I runne into the glead.

XXII: Sestina 1

To every animal that dwells on earth,
Except to those who have in hate the sun,
Their time of labor is while lasts the day;
But when high heaven relumes its thousand stars,
5 This seeks his hut, and that his native wood,
Each finds repose, at least until the dawn.

But I, when fresh and fair begins the dawn
To chase the lingering shades that cloak'd the earth,
Wakening the animals in every wood,
10 No truce to sorrow find while rolls the sun;
And, when again I see the glistening stars,
Still wander, weeping, wishing for the day .

¹ **fowles** birds   ⁶ **wene** think   ¹⁴ **glead** light

When sober evening chases the bright day,
And this our darkness makes for others dawn,
Pensive I look upon the cruel stars   15
Which framed me of such pliant passionate earth,
And curse the day that e'er I saw the sun,
Which makes me native seem of wildest wood.

And yet methinks was ne'er in any wood,
So wild a denizen, by night or day,   20
As she whom thus I blame in shade and sun:
Me night's first sleep o'ercomes not, nor the dawn,
For though in mortal coil I tread the earth,
My firm and fond desire is from the stars.

Ere up to you I turn, oh lustrous stars,   25
Or downwards in love's labyrinthine wood,
Leaving my fleshly frame in moldering earth,
Could I but pity find in her, one day
Would many years redeem, and to the dawn
With bliss enrich me from the setting sun!   30

Oh! might I be with her where sets the sun,
No other eyes upon us but the stars,
Alone, one sweet night, ended by no dawn,
Nor she again transfigured in green wood,
To cheat my clasping arms, as on the day,   35
When Phoebus vainly follow'd her on earth.

I shall lie low in earth, in crumbling wood,
And clustering stars shall gem the noon of day,
Ere on so sweet a dawn shall rise that sun.

[36] **Phoebus** Apollo, whose pursuit of Daphne was "vain" for she
was changed into a laurel (here, as elsewhere, identified with
Laura)

XXVII: Sonnet 23 *

The high successor of our Charles, whose hair
The crown of his great ancestor adorns,
Already has ta'en arms, to bruise the horns
Of Babylon, and all her name who bear;
5   Christ's holy vicar with the honored load
Of keys and cloak, returning to his home,
Shall see Bologna and our noble Rome,
If no ill fortune bar his further road.
Best to your meek and high-born lamb belongs
10   To beat the fierce wolf down: so may it be
With all who loyalty and love deny.
Console at length your waiting country's wrongs,
And Rome's, who longs once more her spouse to see,
And gird for Christ the good sword on thy thigh.

XXX: Sestina 2

I saw beneath the shade of a green laurel
A lady fair and purer than the snow—
And colder too than snow which for long years
Has known no sun. And still that golden hair
5   And lovely face haunt my enraptured eyes
Where'er I wander, on whatever shore.

The ship of my desires will come to shore
Only alas when brown leaves spring from laurel,
When still shall be my heart and dry my eyes;
10   Nay, first we'll see cold fire and flaming snow:
A year shall pass for every thread of hair
Upon my head—and still there will be years.

* For the projected Crusade of 1334, proclaimed by Philip **VI**
of France, son of Charles V   ⁴ **Babylon** the capital of the in-
fidels (Bagdad)   ⁵⁻⁸ refer to the expectation of the Pope's return
to Rome   ⁹⁻¹⁴ probably addressed to the Roman noble Orso
Dell' Anguillara; **lamb** (Italian **agno**) may allude to his wife
Agnese of the Colonna family, enemies of the counts of Tus-
culum whose symbol was a wolf

Aye, but since time so hurries on the years
And soon we all must fare to Charon's shore—
What matter if with blonde or hoary hair?   15
I'll follow faithfully my tender laurel
Through scorching heat or freezing ice and snow
Until the last day close these anxious eyes.

Never has earth beheld such radiant eyes—
Nor in our days nor in the ancient years—   20
As those that vanquish me as summer snow.
A flood of tears, as swollen stream to shore,
Flows from my heart to lave that cruel laurel
Of gleaming limbs and precious golden hair.

Sooner, I fear, shall I change mien and hair   25
Than find some look of pity in the eyes
Of my fair idol, my sweet living laurel.
Today—well counts the heart!—marks seven years
I've wended sighing over sea and shore
By night and day, through rain and sleet and snow.   30

Within afire, without as white as snow
With constant thought though sadly fading hair
I'll go my restless way from shore to shore
Bringing perhaps compassion to some eyes
Who'll read my sorry plaint in future years—   35
If lives the glory of my mortal laurel.

For Laura'll melt my soul as sun melts snow—
Oh hair of gold above bright sapphire eyes!—
And bring my ship of years too soon ashore.

XXXI: Sonnet 24

If that sweet soul, whose early fate I fear,
Called to the other life before her day,
Be so approved above, as well she may,
She will inhabit Heaven's highest sphere.
5 By envy dimmed the sun his front would rear,
Should she within his circle make her stay,
For to behold her beauty's glorious ray,
The chosen souls would flock from far and near.
And in a lower sphere were she to rove
10 For the three lesser lights it were not well,
Since she would filch their glories and their love.
Where Mars has reigned she could not brook to dwell,
And if she higher flew, the star of Jove
And every star that's fixed she would excel.

XXXII: Sonnet 25

Near and yet nearer looms the final day
Setting the finis to my misery.
Time swift and yet more swiftly seems to flee,
Bearing as swiftly all my hopes away.
5 I say to my thoughts: "We shall not long delay
Talking of love together; as we see
The snow, fresh-fallen, vanish suddenly,
So, soon, shall pass the burden of our clay.
And we'll have peace; for with the body dies
10 Hope, the mad agent of our desolation;
And fear dies too, and laughter, wrath, and pain.
Perhaps, from uttermost annihilation,
We'll see some new, strange, marvellous thing arise,
And all our suffering, we shall know, was vain."

⁴ the **highest sphere** is the Empyrean ⁵ the reference is to the sphere of the sun, the fourth of the Ptolemaic heavens ¹⁰ the **three lesser lights** are the spheres of the moon, Mercury and Venus ¹²⁻¹³ the upper spheres are those of Mars, Jupiter, Saturn and the fixed stars

XXXIII: SONNET 26

It was the hour when Venus sent her ray
From orient skies; and still to northward burned
The gentle star that heavenly Juno spurned;
It was the hour when, in the chilly gray,
The barefoot hags arose, their fires to lay,   5
And drowsy spinning-wheels reluctant turned;
It was the hour when dreaming lovers learned
That fancied joy dies with the truthful day.
And in that hour my hope was but a wraith,
Or but a stub of candle, guttering green,   10
When lo! in vision did I see her rise—
Although how changed from that which she had been!—
I heard her say, "How little is your faith!
You'll look again upon these living eyes!"

XXXV: SONNET 28

Alone and ever weary with dark care,
I seek the solitude of desert ways,
Casting about the while a timid gaze
Lest alien steps my refuge seek to share.
No other shield I find against the stare   5
Of curious folk; too clear my face displays
In ashen cheerlessness how cruel the blaze
That burns within, and lays my secret bare.
'Tis only hills, I think, and silent streams
And meadows and deep thickets that can know   10
The tenor of my life, from men concealed.
Yet not so wide I wander with my dreams
But Love comes with me, following where I go,
And long we parley on the lonely weald.

[3] gentle star Ursa Major, the Big Dipper; according to Greek mythology Calisto, beloved of Jupiter, was turned into that constellation to save her from Juno's jealousy

XXXVI: Sonnet 29

If I believed that death could make an end
To love's long torture that has laid me low,
My hand would long ere this have dealt the blow
To summon up oblivion, my friend.
5 But since I fear that I would but descend
From tears to tears, from woe to a worse woe,
On the gulf's edge, with half a step to go,
Irresolute, above the black I bend.
Oh, it were time the pitiless bow were drawn,
10 The cord pulled taut, aim taken carefully,
Time that the shaft into my heart were gone!
Thus I pray Love, and that deaf deity,
Death, whose pale colors I have now put on.
Why is she silent? She has forgotten me.

XL: Sonnet 32 *

If love or death but rend me not asunder—
If I can free me from my binding trap,
The yarn I have for spinning, it may hap,
Will give the century a cause for wonder.
5 The ancient and the new I plan to plunder
And make two truths so neatly overlap
That—dare I say it?—such a mighty clap
I'll make that even in Rome you'll hear it thunder.
However, to embroider my design
10 I need the blessed threading my dear father
Left after him—not all the skein, just some of it.
So be not niggardly; I hate to bother,
Nor is it in your nature to decline;
Be generous—you'll see great things will come of it.

* To Giacomo Colonna   ³ possibly the yarn may be the *Africa*
¹⁰ **my dear father** St. Augustine (?)

XLI: SONNET 33 *

When that fair tree that Phoebus long ago
Once loved in human form, forsakes its site,
Then Vulcan, laboring with all his might,
Shapes fresh sharp arrows for the Olympian's bow.
He then, a-thundering, pours down hail and snow,   5
In scorn of Janus, spurning Caesar's right:
All earth is tear-struck and the sun for spite,
Seeing his love no more, withholds his glow.
Saturn and Mars and armed Orion rise
And cruelly harry hapless barks at sea;   10
Impertinent Aeolus with his lash defies
Neptune and Juno—and humanity,
And all because she briefly from us hides
Whom heavenly choirs one day expect to see.

XLII: SONNET 34

But when, returning, she yields to our sight
Her gentle smile, with charity aglow,
Then vainly in his cavern far below
Dark Aetna, the Sicilian troglodyte
Hammers to shape his master's arms aright,   5
And vainly on the forge his bellows blow;
Meanwhile the beauties of Jove's sister grow
More lovely in Apollo's waxing light.
Zephyr comes forth and reassuringly
Comforts the novice helmsman, pacifies   10
The angry waves, erst driving him to lee;
Ill-boding stars are banished from the skies,
For she, for whom our tears abundantly
Were shed, now looks on us with tender eyes.

* This and the two following sonnets make up a little sequence,
describing the reactions of nature that accompany Laura's de-
parture and return. They are all made on the same rhymes
¹ **fair tree** the laurel (here symbolizing Laura)   ⁶ *i.e.* regardless
of whether it be January or July (Julius Caesar's month)
⁹ **Saturn . . . Mars . . . Orion** storm-bearing stars   ¹¹ **Aeolus**
god of the winds   ¹² **Neptune and Juno** sea and sky   ¹³ **she** Laura

⁴ **Vulcan**   ⁷ **Juno**   ⁸ **Apollo** the Sun god   ⁹ **Zephyr** the West wind

XLIII: Sonnet 35

Nine times with avid glances to and fro
Latona's son had peered from Heaven's height
In search of her whose charms did once excite
His amorous heart, whose grace now others know.
5 But probing near and far and high and low
He found her not; embittered by his plight,
As one half-maddened by uneasy fright
At loss of a dear thing, he fled—and so
He was not there to share my sweet surprise
10 When that dear face appeared again to me
Which yet my pages will immortalize
If heaven grant me so much amnesty;
And while he stood withdrawn, in tears and sighs,
The air retained its dour uncertainty.

L: Ode 5 *

It is the evening hour; the rapid sky
Bends westward; and the hasty daylight flees
To some new land, some strange expectant race.
An old and weary pilgrim-woman sees
5 The lonely foreign desert-dark draw nigh.
Fearful, she urges on her stumbling pace.
And to her resting-place
At length she comes, and knows
The sweetness of repose;
10 The pains of pilgrimage, the road's duress
Fade in enveloping forgetfulness.
But oh, alas, my hurts that ache by day
Are but more pitiless
When the light sinks into the west away.

² **Latona's son** Apollo   ³ **her** Daphne, the laurel, hence Laura

* Composed probably in 1337

When the sun's burning wheels have sped along,   15
And night pursues, rolling its deepest black
From highest peaks into the sheltered plain,
The sober woodsman slings upon his back
His tools, and sings his artless mountain-song,
Discharging on the air his load of pain.   20
And yet his only gain
Is, on his humble board,
The food the woods afford,
Acorns, which poets honor, yet abjure.
Let him be happy, let him sleep secure,   25
Though I no happiness have ever won,
No rest, no ease, no cure,
For all the turning of the stars and sun.

And when the shepherd sees the evening shade
Rising and graying o'er the eastward land,   30
And the sun dropping to its nightly nest,
He rises; takes his well-worn crook in hand;
And leaves the grass, the spring, the beechen glade,
And quietly leads the tired flock to its rest.
He finds a cave, recessed   35
In crags, wherein to spread
Green branches for his bed,
And there he sleeps, untroubled, solitary.
But then, O cruel Love, the more you harry
My breaking strength to that most hopeless chase   40
Of her who flees apace,
And love will never aid to noose the quarry.

In the sea's vales the sailors on their bark
Throw down their limbs on the hard boards to sleep
45 When the sun dips beneath the western main.
Oh, though he hide within the farthest deep,
And leave Morocco's mountains to the dark,
Granada and the Pillars and all Spain,
And though the worldwide pain
50 Of suffering man and beast
In the first night have ceased,
There comes no night with mercy to conclude
My ardor, ever in suffering renewed.
My love grows old; soon shall my captor see me
55 Ten years in servitude.
And still no savior comes with strength to free me!

And as I seek with words my wounds to numb,
I watch at eve the unyoked oxen turning
In from the fields, down from the furrowed hill.
60 My yoke, alas, is never lifted from
My shoulders, and my hurts are ever burning,
And in my eyes the tears are springing still.
Alas, it was my will
To carve the unearthly grace
65 Of her most lovely face
In the immutable matter of my heart.
Now it is carved so deep that strength nor art
May rub it thence until that final day
When soul and body part.
70 Even then, perhaps, it will not pass away.

O my unhappy song,
My grief has made you grieve,
You will not dare to leave
My heart, to show your sorrows anywhere;
And yet, for others' praise you shall not care, 75
For all your burden is the weight of pain
Left by the flames that flare
From the cold rock to which I cling, in vain.

LII: MADRIGAL 1

Diana, naked in the shadowy pool,
Brought no more rapture to the greedy eyes
Of him who watched her splashing in the cool
Than did my glimpse of a maiden unaware
Washing a snood, the gossamer garment of 5
My lady's wild and lovely golden hair;
Wherefore, although the sky burn hot above,
I shake and shiver with a chill of love.

LIII: ODE 6

Generous spirit, who dost rule the frame
Which holds a valiant, wise and skilful lord
During his tenancy of mortal clay;
Since it is thine to wield the honoured sword
Whereby Rome and her wandering sons, made tame, 5
Are led once more along their ancient way,
To thee I call, seeing elsewhere no ray
Of worth, which now the world esteems so low
That men no longer blush at doing wrong.
For what our Italy doth look and long 10
I know not—all unconscious of her woe,
Old, indolent and slow,
She slumbers still, a sleep that none can break—
Would I might grasp her locks and bid her wake.

³ **him** Acteon, for his boldness changed into a stag

¹ **Generous Spirit** for years thought to be Cola di Rienzi; probably Bosone de' Raffaeli da Gubbio, made Roman Senator in 1337

15 I dare not hope, loudly though men may call,
   Her head will lift from such a sluggish trance,
   Whose weary woe sits heavy on her eyes;
   But to thy arms, by fate and not by chance,
   Entrusted is our Rome, our capital,
20 To shake her out of sleep, and bid her rise.
   Thy hand upon the scattered hair that lies
   Across that reverend head fearlessly place
   And draw the sluggard from the mud once more.
   And I, who day and night her grief deplore,
25 In thee along a spark of hope can trace
   That yet the war-god's race
   Relive the glories that their past has known—
   Such years were fitly numbered with thine own.

   Her ancient wall, which still can stir mankind
30 To love and hate, or fill their hearts with dread,
   If but her glorious deeds are told again;
   Her rocky tombs, which hide the mighty dead,
   Whose memory shall never pass from mind
   While the foundations of the world remain;
35 And all who share with them the general bane
   Look for the healing of their wounds to thee.
   Great Scipios, faithful Brutus, could the voice
   Of rumour reach you, how you would rejoice
   At such a wisely placed authority;
40 Nor will the tidings be
   Less welcome to Fabricius, which afford
   A glimpse of Rome's lost beauty now restored.

[20] the Romans identified their founder Romulus with the war
god Quirinus

If heavenly minds are moved by things below,
The souls who left, for this eternal life,
Their bodies to dissolve in earthly mould,   45
Would beg thee end at last the civil strife
Whereby nor peace nor safety now we know,
And many a house is barred, in which of old
The pious pilgrim's vows were often told,
And made a den of lawless thieves, which none   50
Who follow good can enter now, and where
Among dishonoured saints and altars bare
The cruel mandates of the wicked run.
Ah, dire comparison!
For battle now the very bells are rung   55
Which for the praise of God their makers hung.

The weeping women, the defenceless throng
Of babes, the elders, weary of their plight,
Who scorn their life and their superfluous days,
The hooded orders, black and grey and white,   60
And all who travail under pain and wrong,
To thee for help their clamorous voices raise;
The wounds that every frightened wretch displays,
Fearful and numberless, might well inspire
Hannibal's pity, could he gaze on them.   65
But see God's house which now is all aflame—
Couldst thou but quench those sparks which feed the fire,
Then would the wild desire
That burns in every heart be lulled to rest,
And heaven itself account thy labours blest.   70

[60] reference is to Dominicans, Franciscans and Carmelites

Vulture and serpent, lion, wolf and bear,
On a high marble column work their will,
Yet, gnawing it, likewise themselves devour;
Whereat our noble lady, weeping, still
75 Appeals to thee from her domain to tear
The weeds whose rankness never yields a flower.
An age and more divide us from the hour
When Rome was sundered from the chivalry
Which once exalted her; and in its place
80 Today an arrogant and upstart race
Tramples the mighty Mother scornfully.
Her hope is all in thee,
Husband and father both—some other cause
The heavenly Father's care from hers withdraws.

85 Too often high endeavour poorly speeds
Through lack of grudging Fortune's smile, for she
On noblest effort worst reward bestows;
But now that she has cleared a path for thee
I pardon her for all her past misdeeds,
90 Since here at least a better face she shows.
From all that human records can disclose,
The gate of lasting glory never lay
Open so wide to any man before,
For, if I rightly judge, thou canst restore
95 Our noble city to her kingly sway,
And proudly hear men say:
'These served her well when she was young and brave—
He snatched her, old and ailing, from the grave.'

[71] totems denoting respectively the County of Tusculum, the
Gaetani, the Savelli and the Orsini   [72] column the Colonna day

By Mount Tarpeia dwells a chief revered
Through all our land, to whom I send my lay;   100
He prizes others' weal above his own,
Whence I, who never saw, yet long have known
And loved him by repute, am bold to say:
'Thy city, night and day,
From eyes through which her heavy grief distils,   105
Implores thy aid from all her seven hills.'

LVI: SONNET 43

It is the hour—unless my agony
Have shook my wits, my reckoning belying—
It is the hour in pity promised me,
But as I speak, the promised hour is flying.
What shadow chilled the seedling, ripe to free   5
Its spirit into sunny fructifying?
'Twixt hand and grain what wall rose suddenly?
Within the cotes what hungry beast came prying?
I do not know; but this I realize,
That by Love's trickery I have been led.   10
Love! How he dangled joy before my eyes,
Masking the pain he destined for my prize!
What were those wise old words that once I read:
Call no man happy till the day he dies!

[99] **chief** Bosone da Gubbio (?)

LXI: SONNET 47

Blest be the day, and blest the month, the year,
The spring, the hour, the very moment blest,
The lovely scene, the spot, where first oppressed
I sunk, of two bright eyes the prisoner:
5 And blest the first soft pang, to me most dear,
Which thrilled my heart, when Love became its guest;
And blest the bow, the shafts which pierced my brest.
And even the wounds, which bosomed thence I bear.
Blest too the strains which, poured through glade and
     grove,
10 Have made the woodlands echo with her name;
The sighs, the tears, the languishment, the love:
And blest those sonnets, sources of my fame;
And blest that thought—Oh! never to remove!
Which turns to her alone, from her alone which came.

LXII: SONNET 48

O Heavenly Father: after wasted days,
And all these hungry nights when my desire
Ran in my veins with new-replenished fire
At recollection of her lovely ways;
5 O Heavenly Father, lend the hand to raise
Me to the good life whereto I aspire,
Rescue my feet from the encompassing mire
And from the traps my adversary lays.
Father, today the eleventh year is turning
10 Since that unhappy day of desolation
When the yoke first upon my shoulders lay.
Have mercy, Lord, on my long shameful yearning,
Lead thou my thoughts to a better destination,
Remind them, thou wast crucified today.

[9] this would date the sonnet as of 1338

LXVIII: Sonnet 52 *

Your city's holy aspect stirs my sighs
For thinking of the wasted years now past,
Seeming to charge me: 'Wretch, take heed at last,'
And shows my soul the pathway to the skies.
Out springs another thought which that defies   5
And bids my memory rather to hold fast,
Reminding me that e'er much time has passed
I'll look again upon Madonna's eyes.
So, as a man to whom grave news is brought
I listen and am filled with dark dismay—   10
Whereat returning comes the former thought
And drives its foeman from the field away;
Thus bitterly the ceaseless war is fought
Nor can I yet tell who will win the day.

LXXIV: Sonnet 54

I grow a-weary of my wondering .
Why my thoughts never weary, love, of you,
Why I consent to living as I do
Under the burden that my sorrows bring.
Why is it that, for all the songs I sing,   5
I still find words and numbers ever new
For your fair face and eyes—why all night through
'Tis still your name my lips go murmuring?
If, just as after many fruitless days
In your pursuit, for utter weariness   10
My limbs grow stiff, so likewise my poor lays
Have too much ink consumed (as I confess)
And filled too many pages with your praise,
'Tis not for fault of art but Love's excess.

* It is uncertain to whom this sonnet is addressed; Boccaccio
has been suggested. Probably written on the occasion of the
poet's Roman journey of 1336-7

LXXVI: Sonnet 56 *

Love with his promises cajoling me,
To his old prison led me; clapped the door
Upon me, and the keys he handed o'er
To my relentless foe, his votary.
5 Alas, bemused and blind, I could not see
Until too late, their guileful secret war;
And it is only now I come once more,
Struggling and halting, to my liberty.
And though there be an end of prison now,
10 Under familiar chains I still must bend;
I've writ my heart upon my eyes and brow,
And you will read it, you will comprehend.
And seeing my prison pallor, you will vow:
"You've but a little walk to death, my friend."

LXXVII: Sonnet 57 *

That master, Polycletus, and the rest
Whom History boasts, exerting all their art
A thousand years, could only show a part
Of the unrivalled grace that fires my breast;
5 But, surely, Simon, in the regions blessed,
Had seen the beauteous sovereign of my heart,
And thus, among the sons of earth, we start
To see her lineaments so fair expressed.
This face is of some being in the sky,
10 A semblance true; not one, like us, whose soul
Is veiled by cumbrous flesh from every eye:
My friend judged well, who could not form a whole
So various, where, less aided than on high,
The impediments of earth his sight control.

* Written perhaps in 1339

* Written probably in late 1339   [1] **Polycletus** Greek sculptor
of the 5th century B.C.   [5] **Simon** Simon Martini, Sienese painter
(1283-1344), who had painted a portrait of Laura

LXXVIII: Sonnet 58

When that high thought to Simon was conveyed
To which his hand was prompted by the pen
On my behalf, if his choice work had then
Blent voice and reason with the traits displayed,
Then in my breast had many sighs been laid,   5
Through which I slight the things most dear to men;
For peace her aspect seems to pledge me, when
So lowly-hearted she is there portrayed;
And then, when I to talk with her proceed,
I could believe that mildly she gives ear,   10
If to my words she could respond indeed.
Ah but, Pygmalion, how thou shouldst hold dear
That image, if a thousand times thy need
Was helped, by what I long but once to hear!

LXXX: Sestina 4

He that is fast resolved to lead his life
On guileful surges and amid the rocks,
Removed from death by but an inch of wood,
He scarcely can be distant from this end:
And therefore should full soon retire to port,   5
While yet he trusteth helm to govern sail.

The gentle breeze, to which my helm and sail
I trusted, entering on the lover's life,
And hoping I might reach a better port,
Has brought me since to full a thousand rocks,   10
And the first cause of my distressful end
Was not outside, but in that very wood.

¹² Pygmalion fell in love with a statue he had made; Venus
gave it life and the artist married his creation. (Ovid: *Met.* X,
243-97)

⁷ **the gentle breeze** in the original *L'aura* ???? play on Laura

Inclosed a long while in that sightless wood,
I wandered, never lifting eye to sail,
15 Which outwent Fate, and dragged me to my end.
Then pleased it Him, who brought me into life,
To call me so far backward from the rocks,
That I might see, far off at least, the port.

So well was never nightly light in port
20 Discerned from ship or feebler frame of wood,
Though neither tempest intervened, nor rocks,
As I beheld, above my swollen sail,
The lifted banners of yon further life,
And then I fell a-sighing for my end.

25 Nor speak I yet as trusting in my end;
For if I meant to reach by day the port,
Long were the voyage for my span of life.
And still I fear to stand on fragile wood,
And more, than I should wish, inflates my sail
30 That wind, that whilom drove me to the rocks.

Should I with life escape the perilous rocks,
And bring my exile to some calmer end,
How it would make me glad to shift my sail,
And cast my anchor out within some port—
35 Except that I do burn like kindled wood,
So hard's the quitting of my wonted life.

O Lord God of my end and of my life,
Before I split this wood upon the rocks,
Guide thou unto good port my troubled sail.

LXXXI: Sonnet 60

Evil by custom, as by nature frail,
I am so wearied with the long disgrace,
That much I dread my fainting in the race
Should let the original enemy prevail.
Once an Eternal Friend, that heard my cries,   5
Came to my rescue, glorious in his might,
Arm'd with all-conquering love, then took his flight,
That I in vain pursued Him with my eyes.
But his dear words, yet sounding, sweetly say,
"O ye that faint with travel, see the way!   10
Hopeless of other refuge, come to me."
What grace, what kindness, or what destiny
Will give me wings, as the fair-feather'd dove,
To raise me hence and seek my rest above?

LXXXII: Sonnet 61

I've never wearied, love, of loving you,
Nor ever shall while living years endure,
But sharp self-hatred, sorrow without cure,
And tears that spring persistent,—these I rue.
So now the only boon my soul would sue   5
Is your name carven on my sepulture
Beneath whose marble weight my flesh secure
Could find, thus warranted, its rest anew.
Thus, if a living heart may please you still
Without your bruising it, oh then I pray   10
Be kind to mine; if such be not your will
And your disdain is still intent to slay
Or wound your lover, then it chooses ill,
And, thankful, Love and I will go our way.

LXXXIII: Sonnet 62

Till winter's silver frost my temples harrow,
Where shade by shade Time mixes gray with grayer,
Danger will dog me still, ah grim gainsayer,
So long as Love keeps finger upon arrow.
5   Let Love his tortures practice on a sparrow!
I do not dread that treacherous trick-player:
My heart will not fly open for the slayer
To plant his blood-red barbs deep in its marrow!
Mine eyes are stones through which tears cannot blunder,
10 Though well they know the way in, ah so well,
Mountains could not hold tears and eyes asunder!
Even now the flame turns my heart to a hell—
Yet burns not all! Her sinister shape and spell
May trouble, but not trample my sleep under!

LXXXVI: Sonnet 65

Oh, I shall always hate the window whence
Love, idle Love, transfixed me with his ray!
Why had it not sufficient force to slay?
It's good to die in life's young vehemence.
5   No, I must live, in lifelong penitence
Jailed on this earth. What, lifelong, did I say?
My pain will live when life has passed away;
The soul remembers how the heart laments.
Poor soul! You should have learned the lesson well:
10 In vain earth's mightiest do importune
Time to turn back its pages, or suspend
Its flight a moment. There's no more to tell.
Begone, sad soul! He cannot die too soon
Whose happy days have come to their last end.

XC: Sonnet 69

She used to let her golden hair fly free
For the wind to toy and tangle and molest;
Her eyes were brighter than the radiant west.
(Seldom they shine so now.) I used to see
Pity look out of those deep eyes on me.   5
('It was false pity,' you would now protest.)
I had love's tinder heaped within my breast;
What wonder that the flame burned furiously?
She did not walk in any mortal way,
But with angelic progress; when she spoke,   10
Unearthly voices sang in unison.
She seemed divine among the dreary folk
Of earth. You say she is not so today?
Well, though the bow's unbent, the wound bleeds on.

XCI: Sonnet 70

Thy lady fair, whom thou didst love so well,
Hath from amongst us suddenly withdrawn,
And unto heav'n—that dare I hope—is gone;
Such pleasantness and softness round her fell.
'Tis therefore time, that in thy keeping dwell   5
Thy heart's two keys, which living she did own;
Thou shouldst pursue her, by straight path, anon,
And from thee all the weight of earth dispel.
Thou art from thy chief hinderance now freed,
And may'st whate'er remains lay down with ease,   10
And like unloaded pilgrims, may'st emerge.
Thou see'st now well, how every creature flees
Always to death, and how the soul hath need
To step, with lightness, to that perilous verge.

[1] thou probably Petrarch's brother, Gherardo, who after the
death of his lady, entered a Carthusian monastery (1343)

XCII: Sonnet 71

Fair ladies, weep, the while Love's own tears fall;
Ye lovers everywhere, mourn ye for him
Who was the servant of Love's every whim
And made of you his kinsmen, each and all.
5 Now do I fear lest charge of grief appal
My sense and leave unshed these tears that brim,
Or stay the sobs that would shake breast and limb
And bring some solace for this draught of gall.
Oh let the rhymes lament him and the verse:
10 Our Messer Cino, prince of lovers true,
Has but now bidden us his last farewell.
Now may Pistoia and her folk perverse
The loss of their most gentle neighbour rue
And Heaven rejoice where he has gone to dwell.

XCIII: Sonnet 72

Often ere now Love has commanded: "Write,
Write what you've seen in characters of gold;
How I use those whose captive hearts I hold,
Their death in life, their cheeks tear-stained and white.
5 Time was you could right well describe their plight:
Yours was a public fable, widely told;
Then other labors lured you from my fold
But I pursued and caught you in mid flight.
And if those lovely eyes, my citadel,
10 Wherefrom the fatal arrow first was sped
To cleave your carefree heart's obduracy,
Will but return my potent bow to me,
You'll learn you yet have many tears to shed;
Tears are my nourishment, as you know well."

[2] him Cino da Pistoia (1270?-1337?) famous lyric poet, friend of
Dante and Petrarch. A prominent Ghibelline jurist, he was for
a time exiled from his native city

C: Sonnet 79

That window where the sun at midday shows
(Another sun may shine at midnight there);
That other window where the gusty air
Plays chill and wintry tunes when Boreas blows;
That rocky seat whither my lady goes   5
To sit alone and argue with her care;
The stones she's trodden; every pavement where
Her shadow for a second did repose;
That ambush where Love pierced me with his dart;
The new spring season, opening afresh   10
My old, old wounds, after these many years;
Her voice, her words, that wound me in a mesh,
That are today compounded with my heart;
These fill my eyes with a desire of tears.

CI: Sonnet 80

Alas! I know death makes us all his prey,
Nor aught of mercy shows to destined man;
How swift the world completes its circling span,
And faithless Time soon speeds him on his way.
My heart repeats the blast of earth's last day,   5
Yet for its grief no recompense can scan,
Love holds me still beneath its cruel ban,
And still my eyes their usual tribute pay.
My watchful senses mark how on their wing
The circling years transport their fleeter kin,   10
And still I bow enslaved as by a spell:
For fourteen years did reason proudly fling
Defiance at my tameless will, to win
A triumph blest, if Man can good foretell.

⁴ **Boreas** north wind of winter

¹² written then, in 1341

CIII: Sonnet 82 *

Hannibal conquer'd oft, but never knew
The fruits and gain of victory to get,
Wherefore, dear lord, be wise, take care that yet
A like misfortune happen not to you.
5 Still in their lair the cubs and she-bear, who
Rough pasturage and sour in May have met,
With mad rage gnash their teeth and talons whet,
And vengeance of past loss on us pursue:
While this new grief disheartens and appalls,
10 Replace not in its sheath your honour'd sword,
But, boldly following where your fortune calls,
E'en to its goal be glory's path explored,
Which fame and honour to the world may give
That e'en for centuries after death will live.

CIV: Sonnet 83 *

Your virtue, which in bloom we watched of yore,
Where Love commenced with you his first affrays,
A fruit to match that flower now displays,
So that my hope is safely brought ashore.
5 Hence now I'm prompted by my heart to score
Down something, whence your name will gather praise;
For not so firm in marble can one raise
Man's form, that it may stand for evermore.
Caesar, Marcellus, Paulus, Scipio—
10 Do you believe, through aught by anvil done
Or hammer, they'd have ever stood so high?
My Pandolph, as the seasons hurry by,
These works prove fragile, but our art's the one
That doth eternal fame on man bestow.

* Written in May 1333 to encourage Stefano Colonna in his resistance (so far successful) to the Orsini who had attacked him ⁵ she-bear (ital. *orsa*) stands for the house of Orsini; cubs are Bertoldo and Francesco, leaders of the Orsini band

* Addressed (perhaps in 1343) to the famous despot, Pandolfo Malatesta, Lord of Rimini ⁹ Marcellus Roman general who captured Syracuse (212 B.C.); Paulus Emilius victor in the Macedonian War (168 B.C.)

CXII: Sonnet 89

Sennuccio, would you have me, then, confide
My way of life, the tale of my duress?
I burn, I melt, with all the old grievousness,
And Laura rules me still, for, woe betide,
Here she was humble, there she walked in pride,   5
Now harsh, now gentle; pitiful, pitiless;
Now she was gay; now in her sober dress;
Now scornful; now demure; now angry-eyed;
Here she sang sweetly; here she sat awhile;
And here she turned, and there she held her ground;   10
Her eyes here stabbed my heart with a fatal ray;
And here she spoke; and here I saw her smile;
'Twas here she blushed.—Oh, in this helpless round
Our master, Love, pursues me night and day.

CXIV: Sonnet 91 *

Hither from her, whence Shame hath sped away,
And Good hath perished in the evil clime,
From Babel, den of dole and dam of crime,
Fleeing I come, to eke my mortal day.
Alone, as Love admonishes, I stray,   5
Culling now flower and herb, now verse and rhyme,
With meditated hope of better time
Cheering my soul, that there alone finds stay.
Fortune and multitude I nothing mind,
Or much myself, or of poor things have heed,   10
Or burn with outer or with inner heat.
Two souls alone I crave, and would indeed
For her, more gentle mood toward me inclined;
For him, his proved stability of feet.

¹ **Sennuccio del Bene** Florentine poet, friend of Petrarch

* Written possibly in 1342 ⁸ **Babel** Avignon ¹³ **her** Laura
¹⁴ **him** Cardinal Colonna (?) It is uncertain whether **stability of
feet** refers to physical condition or contains a political allegory

CXX: Sonnet 96 *

Those pious verses, which revealed so well
Thy genius and thy generous spirit, so
Inflamed my mind to a responsive glow
That instantly I set about to tell
5 How, though Death has not struck as yet—that knell
None shall escape, that final definite blow—
Nevertheless I too, and with no woe,
Had almost found the gateway to his hell:
But back I came once more because I read
10 Writ large across the lintel that the last
Of my appointed life was not all past,
Though still the ultimate moment's hollow tread
I heard not . . . Therefore be not overcast,
But love that living thou didst praise as dead.

CXXII: Sonnet 97 *

Now seventeen years the circling stars have made
Their journey, since with fire I first was stricken.
Thinking upon my dismal tale, I sicken,
In midst of flame I feel the chill pervade.
5 The saying's true; the wolf has sooner laid
Aside his skin than habit; senses thicken,
Yet all the more the passions blaze and quicken—
Our veil of flesh casts such an evil shade.
Alas! Alas! Shall the day ever be,
10 When the years of ardent life have run their race,
And I emerge from my long trial by fire?
And may I look then, in all honesty,
On the soft beauty of her lovely face,
Untroubled, to the fill of my desire?

* This sonnet is addressed to a poet who had composed a memorial ode for Petrarch, supposing him dead. Written probably in 1343

* April 1344

CXXIII: Sonnet 98

The mist of pallor in such beauteous wise
The sweetness of her smile did overscreen,
That my thrilled heart, upon my visage seen,
Sprang to encounter it in swift surprise.
How soul by soul is scanned in Paradise   5
Then knew I, unto whom disclosed had been
That thought pathetic by all gaze unseen
Save mine, who solely for such sight have eyes.
All look angelical, all tender gest
That e'er on man by grace of woman beamed   10
At side of this had shown discourtesy.
The gentle visage, modestly deprest
Earthward, inquired with silence, as meseemed,
"Who draws my faithful friend away from me?"

CXXVI: Ode 14 *

Clear, fresh, and dulcet streams
Which the fair shape, who seems
To me sole woman, haunted at noontide;
Fair bough, so gently fit,
(I sigh to think of it,)   5
Which lent a pillar to her lovely side;
And turf, and flowers bright-eyed,
O'er which her folded gown
Flow'd like an angel's down;
And you, oh holy air and hush'd,   10
Where first my heart at her sweet glances gush'd;
Give ear, give ear, with one consenting,
To my last words, my last and my lamenting.

* Composed 1343 (?)

If 'tis my fate below
15 And Heaven will have it so,
That Love must close these dying eyes in tears,
May my poor dust be laid
In middle of your shade,
While my soul, naked, mounts to its own spheres.
20 The thought would calm my fears,
When taking, out of breath,
The doubtful step of death;
For never could my spirit find
A stiller port after the stormy wind;
25 Nor in more calm, abstracted bourne,
Slip from my travail'd flesh, and from my bones outworn.

Perhaps, some future hour
To her accustom'd bower
Might come the untamed, and yet the gentle she;
30 And where she saw me first,
Might turn with eyes athirst
And kinder joy to look again for me;
Then, oh, the charity,
Seeing amidst the stones
35 The earth that held my bones,
A sigh for very love at last
Might ask of Heaven to pardon me the past:
And Heaven itself could not say nay,
As with her gentle veil she wiped the tears away.

How well I call to mind,   40
When from those boughs the wind
Shook down upon her bosom flower on flower;
And there she sat, meek-eyed,
In midst of all that pride,
Sprinkled and blushing through an amorous shower.   45
Some to her hair paid dower,
And seem'd to dress the curls,
Queenlike, with gold and pearls;
Some, snowing, on her drapery stopp'd,
Some on the earth, some on the water dropp'd;   50
While others, fluttering from above,
Seem'd wheeling round in pomp, and saying, 'Here reigns
    Love.'

How often then I said,
Inward, and filled with dread,
'Doubtless this creature came from Paradise!'   55
For at her look the while,
Her voice, and her sweet smile,
And heavenly air, truth parted from mine eyes;
So that, with long-drawn sighs,
I said, as far from men,   60
'How came I here, and when?'
I had forgotten; and alas!
Fancied myself in heaven, not where I was;
And from that time till this, I bear
Such love for the green bower, I can not rest elsewhere. 65

If thouds't apparel as thou hast good will,
Thou couldst have boldly broke
Out from the woods, and gone amidst the folk.

CXXVIII: Ode 16 *

Oh, my own Italy! though words are vain
The mortal wounds to close,
Unnumber'd, that thy beauteous bosom stain,
Yet may it soothe my pain
5 To sigh forth Tyber's woes,
And Arno's wrongs, as on Po's sadden'd shore
Sorrowing I wander, and my numbers pour.
Ruler of heaven! By the all-pitying love
That could thy Godhead move
10 To dwell a lowly sojourner on earth,
Turn, Lord! on this thy chosen land thine eye:
See, God of Charity!
From what light cause this cruel war has birth;
And the hard hearts by savage discord steel'd,
15 Thou, Father! from on high,
Touch by my humble voice, that stubborn wrath may
     yield!

Ye, to whose sovereign hands the fates confide
Of this fair land the reins,—
(This land for which no pity wrings your breast)—
20 Why does the stranger's sword her plains invest?
That her green fields be dyed,
Hope ye, with blood from the Barbarians' veins?
Beguiled by error weak,
Ye see not, though to pierce so deep ye boast,
25 Who love, or faith, in venal bosoms seek:
When throng'd your standards most,
Ye are encompass'd most by hostile bands.
Oh hideous deluge gather'd in strange lands,
That rushing down amain
30 O'erwhelms our every native lovely plain!
Alas! if our own hands
Have thus our weal betray'd, who shall our cause sustain?

* Composed either in 1345, during a war between the Gonzaga
and Este families for the possession of Parma, or in 1354 during
hostilities between Genoa and Venice

29 **hideous deluge** bands of foreign mercenaries

Well did kind Nature, guardian of our state,
Rear her rude Alpine heights,
A lofty rampart against German hate;   35
But blind ambition, seeking his own ill,
With ever restless will,
To the pure gales contagion foul invites:
Within the same strait fold
The gentle flocks and wolves relentless throng,   40
Where still meek innocence must suffer wrong:
And these,—oh shame avow'd!—
Are of the lawless hordes no tie can hold:
Fame tells how Marius' sword
Erewhile their bosoms gored,—   45
Nor has Time's hand aught blurr'd the record proud!
When they who, thirsting, stoop'd to quaff the flood,
With the cool waters mix'd, drank of a comrade's blood!

Great Caesar's name I pass, who o'er our plains
Pour'd forth the ensanguin'd tide,   50
Drawn by our own good swords from out their veins;
But now—nor know I what ill stars preside—
Heaven holds this land in hate!
To you the thanks!—whose hands control her helm!
You, whose rash feuds despoil   55
Of all the beauteous earth the fairest realm!
Are ye impell'd by judgment, crime, or fate,
To oppress the desolate?
From broken fortunes, and from humble toil,
The hard-earn'd dole to wring,   60
While from afar ye bring
Dealers in blood, bartering their souls for hire?
In truth's great cause I sing,
Nor hatred nor disdain my earnest lay inspire.

Marius the Roman general who defeated the Germans at
Aquae Sextiae (102 B.C.)

65 Nor mark ye yet, confirm'd by proof on proof,
 Bavaria's perfidy,
 Who strikes in mockery, keeping death aloof?
 (Shame, worse than aught of loss, in honor's eye?)
 While ye, with honest rage, devoted pour
70 Your inmost bosom's gore!—
 Yet give one hour to thought,
 And ye shall own how little he can hold
 Another's glory dear who sets his own at nought.
 Oh, Latin blood of old!
75 Arise, and wrest from obloquy thy fame,
 Nor bow before a name
 Of hollow sound, whose power no laws enforce!
 For if barbarians rude
 Have higher minds subdued,
80 Ours! ours the crime!—not such wise Nature's course.

 Ah! is not this the soil my foot first press'd?
 And here, in cradled rest,
 Was I not softly hush'd?—here fondly rear'd?
 Ah! is not this my country?—so endear'd
85 By every filial tie?
 On whose lap shrouded both my parents lie!
 Oh, by this tender thought,
 Your torpid bosoms to compassion wrought,
 Look on the people's grief!
90 Who, after God, of you expect relief;
 And if ye but relent,
 Virtue shall rouse her in embatted might,
 Against blind fury bent,
 Nor long shall doubtful hang the unequal fight;
95 For no,—the ancient flame
 Is not extinguish'd yet, that raised the Italian name!

 [66] The perfidy refers to the habit of the mercenaries, often
Germans, of merely pretending to fight for their Italian masters

Mark, sovereign Lords! how Time, with pinions strong,
Swift hurries life along!
E'en now, behold! Death presses on the rear.
We sojourn here a day—the next, are gone!   100
The soul disrobed—alone,
Must shuddering seek the doubtful pass we fear.
Oh, at the dreaded bourne,
Abase the lofty brow of wrath and scorn,
(Storms adverse to the eternal calm on high!)   105
And ye, whose cruelty
Has sought another's harm, by fairer deed
Of heart, or hand, or intellect, aspire
To win the honest meed
Of just renown—the noble mind's desire!   110
Thus sweet on earth the stay!
Thus to the spirit pure, unbarr'd is Heaven's way!

My song! with courtesy, and numbers sooth,
Thy daring reasons grace,
For thou the mighty, in their pride of place,   115
Must woo to gentle ruth,
Whose haughty will long evil customs nurse,
Ever to truth averse!
Thee better fortunes wait,
Among the virtuous few—the truly great!   120
Tell them—but who shall bid my terrors cease?
Peace! Peace! on thee I call! return, oh heaven-born
    Peace!

CXXIX: Ode 17 *

From thought to thought, from mountain peak to mountain
Love leads me on; for I can never still
My trouble on the world's well-beaten ways.
If on a barren heath there springs a fountain,
5 Or a dark valley huddles under a hill,
There may the grieving soul find quiet days;
There freely she obeys
Love's orders, laughing, weeping, hoping, fearing,
And the face writes a gloss upon the soul,
10 Now glad, now charged with dole,
Not long in any manner persevering.
At sight of me a man of subtle wit
Would say, "He burns, and sees no end of it."

In the high mountains, in the woods I find
15 A little solace; every haunt of man
Is to my mood a mortal enemy.
At every step a new thought comes to mind
Of my dear lady, whose remembrance can
Turn all the hurt of love to gayety.
20 I would no sooner be
Quit of this bittersweet existence here,
Than I reflect, "Yet even now Love may
Destine the better day;
I, loathing self, may be to others dear!"
25 So I go thinking, hoping, sighing, now;
May it be true indeed? And when? And how?

* Composed it would seem in 1345

And in the shade of a pine tree on a hill
I halt, and all the tumbled rocks near by
Are pictured with the beauty of her face;
And tears of tender melancholy fill   30
My bosom; and "Alas! alas!" I cry,
"What have I come to! From how far a place!"
But, for the little space
That the uneasy mind thus looks on her,
Rapt out of self into another sphere,   35
Then I feel Love so near
That the tricked soul rejoices it should err.
So clear I see her, and so fair and pure
That I pray only that the fraud endure.

Often I've seen her—who'll believe me now?—   40
Treading the grass, cleaving the lucid water,
Alive, alive, in a forest beech-trunk caught,
White mid the clouds; so fair, Leda would vow
The famous beauty of her lovely daughter
Is dimmed as a star when the broad sun beams hot.   45
And, in what savage spot
I chance to be, in what most barren shore,
Ever more beautiful she walks with me.
Then, when Truth makes to flee
My darling cheat, I find my self once more   50
A dead stone statue, set on living stone,
Of one who thinks and grieves and writes alone.

" Leda's daughter was Helen of Troy

Now it's my whole desire and all my pleasure
Up to the highest mountain-pass to climb
55 To dizzy and unshadowed solitude.
And thence I send my flying gaze to measure
My length of woe; I weep a little time;
The mist of grief blows from my dismal mood.
I stare afar and brood
60 On the leagues that lie between me and that face,
Ever so near and yet so far away.
Soft to myself I say,
"My soul, be brave; perhaps, in that far place,
She thinks of you in absence, and she sighs!"
65 And my soul suddenly wakes and gladly cries.

My song, beyond these alps,
In the land where skies are gladder and more clear,
You'll see me soon, where a quick streamlet flows,
And where the fragrance blows
70 Of the fresh Laurel that I love so dear.
There is my heart, and she who reft it me;
Here you may see only my effigy.

CXXXI: Sonnet 101

I'd sing such songs of love, that every day
I'd draw a thousand sighs from that hard breast;
A thousand high desires, that lie unguessed
Within, would warm and bloom in ardent May.
5 And pity upon her lovely face would play,
Her eyes, tear-wet with sorrow, would attest
That all-too-late regrets of one distressed
By the afflictions of a mistaken way.
I'd see the snowbound roses of her lips
10 Quivering; and that glint of ivory
That marbles the onlooker; every reason
I'd see wherefor my joy of life outstrips
The pain of it; I shout exultantly
That I am kept into this elder season.

CXXXII: SONNET 102

If no love is, O god, what fele I so?
And if love is, what thing and whiche is he?
If love be good, from whennes comth my wo?
If it be wikke, a wonder thinketh me,
When every torment and adversitee   5
That cometh of him, may to me savory thinke;
For ay thurst I, the more that I it drinke.

And if that at myn owene lust I brenne,
Fro whennes cometh my wailing and my pleynte?
If harme agree me, wher-to pleyne I thenne?   10
I noot, ne why unwery that I feynte.
O quike deeth, o swete harm so queynte,
How may of thee in me swich quantitee,
But-if that I consente that it be?

And if that I consente, I wrongfully   15
Compleyne, y-wis; thus possed to and fro,
Al sterelees with-inne a boot am I
A-mid the see, by twixen windes two,
That in contrarie stonden ever-mo.
Allas! what is this wonder maladye?   20
For hete of cold, for cold of hete, I dye.

⁴ **thinketh** it seems ⁶ **savory:** pleasant ⁸ **lust** will **brenne** burn
¹⁰ **agree** please ¹¹ **noot** know not ¹² **quicke:** living; **queynte**
strange ¹⁴ **but-if** unless ¹⁶ **y-wis** truly; **possed:** tossed ¹⁷ **stere-
lees** ruderless, **boot** boat ²⁰ **wonder** strange

CXXXIV: Sonnet 104

I find no peace and bear no arms for war,
I fear, I hope; I burn yet shake with chill;
I fly the Heavens, huddle to earth's floor,
Embrace the world yet all I grasp is nil.
5 Love opens not nor shuts my prison's door
Nor claims me his nor leaves me to my will;
He slays me not yet holds me evermore,
Would have me lifeless yet bound to my ill.
Eyeless I see and tongueless I protest,
10 And long to perish while I succor seek;
Myself I hate and would another woo.
I feed on grief, I laugh with sob-racked breast
And death and life alike to me are bleak:
My Lady, thus I am because of you.

CXXXVI: Sonnet 105 *

Vengeaunce must fall on thee, thow filthie whore
Of Babilon, thow breaker of Christ's fold,
That from achorns, and from the water colde,
Art riche become with making many poore.
5 Thow treason's neste that in thie harte dost holde
Of cankard malice, and of myschief more
That pen can wryte, or may with tongue be tolde,
Slave to delights that chastitie hath solde;
For wyne and ease which settith all thie store
10 Uppon whoredome and none other lore,
In thye pallais of strompetts yonge and olde
Theare walks Plentie, and Belzebub thye Lorde
Guydes thee and them, and doth thye raigne upholde:
It is but late, as wryting will recorde,
15 That poore thow weart withouten lande or goolde;
Yet how hath golde and pryde, by one accorde,
In wichednesse so spreadd thie lyf abrode,
That it dothe stincke before the face of God.

* Against the corruption of the Papal Court in Avignon; perhaps
written in 1347; clearly cxxxviii is of the same period

CXXXVIII: Sonnet 107

Spring of all woe, O den of curssed ire,
Scoole of errour, temple of heresye;
Thow Pope, I meane, head of hypocrasye,
Thow and thie churche, unsaciat of desyre,
Have all the world filled full of myserye;   5
Well of desceate, thow dungeon full of fyre,
That hydes all truthe to breed idolatrie.
Thow wicked wretche, Chryste cannot be a lyer,
Behold, therefore, thie judgement hastelye;
Thye first founder was gentill povertie,   10
But there against is all thow dost requyre.
Thow shameless beaste wheare hast thow thie trust,
In thie whoredome, or in thie riche attyre?
Loe! Constantyne, that is turned into dust,
Shall not retourne for to mayntaine thie lust;   15
But now his heires, that might nor sett thee higher,
For thie greate pryde shall teare thye seate asonder,
And scourdge thee so that all the world shall wonder.

CXL: Sonnet 109

Loue, that liueth, and reigneth in my thought,
That built his seat within my captiue brest,
Clad in the armes, wherein with me he fought,
Oft in my face he doth his banner rest.
She, that me taught to loue, and suffer payne,   5
My doubtfull hope, and eke my hote desyre,
With shamefast cloke to shadowe, and refraine,
Her smiling grace conuerteth straight to yre.
And coward Loue then to the hart apace
Taketh his flight, whereas he lurkes, and plaines   10
His purpose lost, and dare not shewe his face.
For my lordes gilt thus faultlesse byde I paynes.
Yet from my lorde shall not my foote remoue.
Swete is his death, that takes his end by loue.

---

[4] **unsaciat** insatiable   [14] **Constantine,** whose famous "donation"
was believed to have given the western world to the church

[12] **byde I paynes** I suffer

CXLV: Sonnet 113 *

Ah set me where the sun sears blade and flowers,
Or where his ardor struggles with the snows,
Or in the zones where he more justly glows,
Where he is caught, where yielded by the Hours.
5 In weather fair, 'midst angry storms and showers,
In low estate or high as mankind knows,
In daytime, long or short, when shadows close;
In pride of youth or when senescence lowers;
On earth, in heaven or in a deep ravine,
10 High on a hill or in the lowland mire,
In living flesh or as a spirit clean;
Unknown to fame or such that all admire—
I'll live as I have lived these past fifteen
Devoted years, still tuning my sad lyre.

CXLVI: Sonnet 114

Fair Spirit, with all virtue fired and crowned,
For whom my pen so long inscribes my lays,
Dwelling of Fair Report from girlish days,
Tower based on worth transcendent and profound!
5 O flame! O rose in teeming leaves unbound
Of living snow, sole pattern of my gaze!
Rapture, whence urged my soaring wing I raise
To fairer light than else 'neath Heaven is found!
From Thule unto Calpe hymned should be
10 Thy name, in Bactrian, Indian, Scythian ear
Resounded, rang so far this lyre of mine:
But, this forbidden, the fair land shall hear,
Begirt by wall of Alp and azure sea,
And cloven by the ridges Apennine.

* Written probably in 1342, as line 13 indicates

⁹ **Thule** northern island of legend, possibly Iceland **Calpe** one
of the "pillars of Hercules" that mark the strait of Gibraltar
¹⁰ **Bactria** a region of Asiatic Scythia ¹² **the fair land** Italy

CXLVIII: Sonnet 116

No Tessin,Tiber, Adige, Arno, Po,
Euphrates, Tigris, Indus, Ganges, Don,
Alphaeus, Hermus, Hebrus, Var, Garonne,
Rhone, Rhine, Elbe, Ebro, Seine, sea's rending flow—
No ivy, fir, beech, juniper, the glow   5
Could mitigate, which through my sad heart's gone—
Like one fair stream, my sorrow's mate, whereon
Those leaves, my rhymes have decked and lauded, grow.
A refuge here I find in Love's onslaughts,
Which have in arms compelled me still to live   10
The life, that past me springs in eager flight.
Long on green bank, fair laurel, mayst thou thrive,
And may thy planter high chivalrous thoughts,
In the sweet shade and water's murmurs, write.

CXLIX: Ballata 6

From time to time more clemency for me
In that sweet smile and angel form I trace;
Seem too her lovely face
And lustrous eyes at length more kind to be.
Yet, if thus honour'd, wherefore do my sighs   5
In doubt and sorrow flow,
Signs that too truly show
My anguish'd desperate life to common eyes?
Haply if, where she is, my glance I bend,
This harass'd heart to cheer,   10
Methinks that Love I hear
Pleading my cause, and see him succour lend.
Not therefore at an end the strife I deem,
Nor in sure rest my heart at last esteem;
For Love most burns within   15
When hope most pricks us on the way to win.

[7] **fair stream** the Sorgue, flowing past Vaucluse   [8] **those leaves**
allude to a laurel the poet had planted in honor of Laura

CL: Sonnet 117

"What are you thinking, soul? And shall we see
This war forever? Shall no truce occur?"
"Why, who can tell our fate? But I'll aver
She likes not our disease, Fidelity."
5 "And what of that, if but by glancing, she
May make us fire, or than ice icier?"
"That is the work of Love; no blame to her."
"Why speaks she then no word to set us free?"
"Sometimes the tongue is silent, and the heart
10 Laments in misery; the tearless eyes
Laugh, hiding floods of anguish past belief."
"Little indeed such comfort satisfies
The mind where stagnant sorrows lurk and smart!
Hope is incredible to the slave of grief."

CLIII: Sonnet 120

Go, my warm sighs, go to that frozen breast,
Burst the firm ice, that charity denies;
And, if a mortal prayer can reach the skies,
Let death or pity give my sorrows rest!
5 Go, softest thoughts! Be all you know express'd
Of that unnoticed by her lovely eyes,
Though fate and cruelty against me rise,
Error at least and hope shall be repress'd.
Tell her, though fully you can never tell,
10 That, while her days calm and serenely flow,
In darkness and anxiety I dwell;
Love guides your flight, my thoughts securely go,
Fortune may change, and all may yet be well!
If my sun's aspect not deceives my woe.

CLVI: Sonnet 123

I saw angelic gest in earthly spheres,
And heavenly beauty paralleled of none,
Which now I joy and grieve to think upon,
Since now all else dream, shadow, smoke appears.
And twin lights have I seen obscured by tears,   5
Lights which so oft gave envy to the Sun:
Mount well might move and stream forget to run,
Heard they the sounds that smote upon these ears.
Love, wisdom, valour, tenderness, and grief
Weeping together made more sweet consent   10
Than any wonted on wide earth to sound;
Harmony holding heaven so intent
That not on any branch moved any leaf,
By such enchantment air and wind were bound.

CLIX: Sonnet 126

In what divine ideal, what lofty sphere
Is found the pattern from which Nature made
That face so fair wherein she might parade
Proof of her heavenly power to mortals here?
Were ringlets ever loosed of gold more sheer   5
To wayward breeze by nymph in pool or glade?
Was every virtue in one soul displayed
Ere now?—and how the noblest cost me dear!
Who knows her not can never realize
How beauty may the heart of man beguile,   10
And who looks not upon my Laura's eyes
Knows not how love can kill and otherwhile
May heal us; let him hear how soft she sighs
And gently speaks, oh, let him see her smile!

CLX: Sonnet 127

Love and I stood agape; we marvelled how
No wonder's ever mazed the human sight
Like the speaking lips and laughing eyes alight
Of our one Lady, who has no equal now.
5 Under the fair serene of her calm brow
My ruling constant stars are shining bright
To fire the kindred heart and lead aright
Him who would take Love's last, severest vow.
It is a miracle, when in the grass
10 Like a flower she sits! Or when her candid breast
Is crushed against a bush, without her care!
How sweet it is, in Spring to see her pass
Alone, and by her lovely thoughts caressed,
Weaving a circlet for her golden hair!

CLXI: Sonnet 128

O wandering steps! O vague and busy dreams!
O changeless memory! O fierce desire!
O passion strong! heart weak with its own fire;
O eyes of mine! not eyes, but living streams;
5 O laurel boughs! whose lovely garland seems
The sole reward that glory's deeds require!
O haunted life! delusion sweet and dire,
That all my days from slothful rest redeems;
O beauteous face! where Love has treasured well
10 His whip and spur, the sluggish heart to move
At his least will; nor can it find relief.
O souls of love and passion! if ye dwell
Yet on this earth, and ye, great Shades of Love!
Linger, and see my passion and my grief.

CLXIII: Sonnet 130

Love, who dost every thought of mine behold,
And rugged ways where thou alone dost guide,
By thee be secrets of my heart espied,
Locked from all other gaze, to thine unrolled,
Thou knowest what chase of thee hath cost of old,   5
Yet day by day from steep to steep dost glide,
Nor heedest how thy comrade from thy side
Roughness of way and weary foot withhold.
True, I descry from far the gentle ray
Whereto to urge me on thou hast intent,   10
But have not wings, alas! like thee to fly.
Desire it shall sufficiently content
To wear in languishing my life away,
Nor work my Love displeasure by my sigh.

CLXIV: Sonnet 131

Now while the wind and earth and heavens rest,
While sleep holds beast and feathered bird in fee,
And high above a calm and waveless sea
The silent stars obey the night's behest,
I lie awake and yearning, sore distressed   5
Tortured by thoughts of my sweet enemy;
And though her face recalled brings death to me
'Tis only with such dreams I soothe my breast.
So from one living fountain, gushing clear,
Pour forth alike the bitter and the sweet,   10
And one same hand can deal me good or ill;
Whence every day I die anew of fear
And live again to learn that hope's a cheat,
So peace of heart or mind escapes me still.

CLXV: Sonnet 132

Emerald and alabaster mingle where
She walks the meadow grass in comely wise,
And round her footsoles livelier colours rise
From flowers that find reviving virtue there.
5 Love, which for gentle spirits spreads his snare,
Nor on the grosser sort his cunning plies,
Rains such warm rapture from these beauteous eyes
That for no bliss or nurture else I care.
Fair as her gait and as her gentle brow
10 Is her melodious voice, and she doth link
A modest mien with actions mild and slow.
From these four sparks, nor these alone, I think
Springs the great flame, within whose furnace glow
Consumed, like nightbirds from the sun, I shrink.

CLXVIII: Sonnet 135

Love sends me messenger of gentle thought,
Since days of yore our trusty go-between,
And comforts me, who ne'er, he saith, have been
So near as now to hope's fruition brought.
5 I, who the lore he redeth ever fraught
With intermingled truth and lies have seen,
Abide perplexed, uncertain what to ween,
'Twixt doubtful Yes and doubtful No distraught.
So speed the hours, and I meanwhile in glass
10 See myself speeding too where years deny
Fulfilment of his promise and my hope.
So be it, years of others also pass;
Life's onward march puts not my passion by,
But frights me with its brief remaining scope.

CLXXII: Sonnet 139

O envy, virtue's constant nemesis,
Breathing hot challenge to the sweet and fine!
By what soft stealth, furtive and serpentine,
Have you gained ingress, changed her into this?
You have uprooted thence my deepest bliss,   5
Showing me, in this happier love than mine,
How she, that once bestowed such looks benign,
Seems cold now, coiled for a perpetual hiss.
Yet though, by subtle little cruelties,
You grudge my good and sneer at my distress,   10
You cannot alter one thought, if you please!
Not though a thousand times each day confess
Her scorn, nor hope nor love grows less by these,
Her threats are nothing: Love survives the stress.

CLXXIV: Sonnet 141

If, as some deem, from stars man's fate is shed,
Cruel the star that on my birth did glow,
Cruel the cot that rocked me for my woe,
Cruel the earth that I grew up to tread;
And cruel from whose eyes the arrow fled   5
To pierce me, target pitched but for her bow;
My hurt eftsoons I flew to thee to show,
Love, who could'st heal it with the bolt thus sped.
But thou dost make thy pleasure of my pain;
Not she, who chides that but of arrow is,   10
And not of spear, the wound for which I grieve.
But I take comfort, weening to be fain
For her, than joy with others better bliss.
Thou swear'st this by thy shaft, and I believe.

CLXXVI: Sonnet 143 *

Through savage woods I walk without demur
Where men well-armed might hesitate to fare,
What shall I fear who long since learned to bear
Those love-charged glances that my pulses stir?
5 Boldly I tread and sing the praise of her
Whom Heaven could not from my bosom tear,
Nay, for I see her semblance everywhere
In fancied shape of looming beech or fir.
In the sweet melody by wood things chorus'd
10 I seem to hear her: in the quivering leaf,
The rippling brook, the thrush's plaintive note.
Ah dear to me the wildness of the forest
And sweet its solitude past all belief—
Were not my only sun too far remote.

CLXXVIII: Sonnet 145

Love plies me with the spur, tugs on the bit,
Emboldens and affrights, now hot, now freezing,
Invites, rejects, and threatens while appeasing,
Extends fair hopes, then shows them counterfeit,
5 Flies up, swoops low and ever bears with it,
Unsatisfied with what it should find pleasing,
My weary heart, sick of capricious teasing,
Well matched with misled and bewildered wit.
A sympathetic thought points out the ford
10 Across a stream—not that of tears outwelling—
To lead me to a peace I've never known,
But then, as yielding to a stronger lord
I seek another path, resigned to dwelling
Where I must find my heart's death—and my own.

* Written in 1333 after a journey from Cologne through the Ardennes forest

CLXXIX: Sonnet 146 *

Geri, whenever my sweet, lovely foe,
That is so haughty, gets displeased with me,
There is but one resource, that sets me free
From death, and lets my soul draw breath in woe.
Wherever she may looks indignant throw   5
That quite bereft of light my life may be,
I let her mine so truly humble see
That she perforce must all disdain forego.
Were it not thus, I could no more draw near
Her presence than I could Medusa's face,   10
Which all beholders turned to alabaster.
Do thou then likewise, for I see no place
For other acts; and flight is bootless here
Before such pinions, as transport our master.

CLXXX: Sonnet 147

River, this husk of me well mayest thou
Bear on thy fleet and potent flood away,
But the free soul these veils of flesh array
Not to thy might or other might doth bow.
Scorning all shifts of sail or helm or prow,   5
Direct on favouring breeze she takes her way;
Wind wave and sheet and oar her nothing stay,
Bound upon beating wing to golden bough.
Po, king of rivers, first in pride and might,
Encountering the sun when day he leads,   10
And fairer light forsaking in the West;
'Tis but my earthly part thy torrent speeds:
The other, in soft plumes of Love bedight,
Wings back her way to her beloved nest.

* Written in reply to a sonnet of Geri de' Gianfigliazzi, a
Florentine poet

* Perhaps written in 1345, recording a boat trip from Parma to
Verona

CLXXXV: Sonnet 152

This Phoenix, from her wealth of aureate plumes
Sheathing her snowy neck in splendid dyes,
Hath natural necklace fashioned in a wise
That softens other hearts, and mine consumes.
5 And all around this diadem illumes
The airy space, while Love his bellows plies,
And silent bids the subtle flame arise
That scorches me mid winter's chills and glooms.
A purple scarf, with fringing roses sown
10 O'er bordering blue, her snowy shoulders veils;
Garb like her beauty to none other given:
In aromatic Araby alone
Fame plants this prodigy, with idle tales
Concealing that she soars in our own heaven.

CLXXXVI: Sonnet 153

Had tuneful Maro seen, and Homer old,
The living sun which here mine eyes behold,
The best powers they had join'd of either lyre,
Sweetness and strength, that fame she might acquire:
5 Unsung had been, with vex'd Aeneas, then
Achilles and Ulysses, godlike men,
And for nigh sixty years who ruled so well
The world; and who before Aegysthus fell;
Nay, that old flower of virtues and of arms,
10 As this new flower of chastity and charms,
A rival star, had scarce such radiance flung.
In rugged verse him honour'd Ennius sung,
I her in mine. Grant, Heaven! on my poor lays
She frown not, nor disdain my humble praise.

[1] **Phoenix** legendary bird of Arabia, said to live 500 years, burn, and be reborn from its own ashes

[1] **Maro** Virgil [7] **who ruled** Augustus [8] **who . . . fell** Agammemnon, slain by Aegysthus, his wife's lover [9] **old flower** Scipio Africanus celebrated by the poet Ennius [10] **new flower** Laura

CLXXXVIII: Sonnet 155

O nurturing Sun, that leaf of all my love,
First loved by thee, in her sweet earth alone
Blossoms unparalleled since, all unknown,
On Adam burst the splendour men dream of.
O pause to gaze at her! Though I approve   5
And do entreat thy dalliance, thou art flown—
Or poised for flight: the mountain dusk is down,
The day beneath proud fillets doth remove.
The shadows from those gentle mountains falling,
Where sparkles my sweet fire, where bravely grew   10
That noble laurel from a shoot or two—
Those shadows grow more dense, as I speak, walling
From sight the lovely landscape, the dear view,
My true Queen's castle where my heart is calling.

CLXXXIX: Sonnet 156

Charged with oblivion my ship careers
Through stormy combers in the depth of night;
Left lies Charybdis, Scylla to the right;
My master—nay, my foe sits aft and steers.
Wild fancies ply the oars, mad mutineers,   5
Reckless of journey's end or tempest's might;
The canvas splits 'gainst the relentless spite
Of blasts of hopes and sighs and anxious fears.
A rain of tears, a blinding mist of wrath
Drench and undo the cordage, long since worn   10
And fouled in knots of ignorance and error;
The two sweet lights are lost that showed my path,
Reason and art lie 'neath the waves forlorn:
What hope of harbor now? I cry in terror.

[3] **Charybdis, Scylla** mythical monsters symbolizing the two
shores of the strait of Messina, noted for its storms

CXCII: Sonnet 159

Stand we here, Love, our glory to survey;
Things Nature over passing, wondrous, new;
Behold what sweet of her doth Earth imbue;
Behold what light in her doth Heaven display.
5 See Art impearl, impurple, gild the array
Of mortal charms none other may indue;
See her feet traverse and her eyes review
The cloistered vales of her enshadowed way.
Herbage and troops of many-tinted flowers
10 Sprinkled beneath yon old dark ilex-stem
Pray for her tender foot's imprinted trace:
And starry sparks, alit as evening lowers,
Throb mid transparent skies that joy with them
To image the sereneness of her face.

CXCV: Sonnet 162 *

I alter day by day in hair and mien,
Yet shun not the old dangerous baits and dear,
Nor sever from the laurel, limed and green,
Which nor the scorching sun, nor fierce cold sear.
5 Dry shall the sea, the sky be starless seen,
Ere I shall cease to covet and to fear
Her lovely shadow, and—which ill I screen—
To like, yet loathe, the deep wound cherished here:
For never hope I respite from my pain,
10 From bones and nerves and flesh till I am free,
Unless mine enemy some pity deign,
Till things impossible accomplished be,
None but herself or death the blow can heal
Which Love from her bright eyes has left my heart to feel.

* Composed possibly in 1342, perhaps for the anniversary of his
enamorment

CXCVI: Sonnet 163

The gentle gale, that plays my face around,
Murmuring sweet mischief through the verdant grove,
To fond remembrance brings the time, when Love
First gave his deep, although delightful wound;
Gave me to view that beauteous face, ne'er found   5
Veil'd, as disdain or jealousy might move;
To view her locks that shone bright gold above,
Then loose, but now with pearls and jewels bound:
Those locks she sweetly scatter'd to the wind,
And then coil'd up again so gracefully,   10
That but to think on it still thrills the sense.
These Time has in more sober braids confined;
And bound my heart with such a powerful tie,
That death alone can disengage it thence.

CXCIX: Sonnet 166

O lovely hand that lightly holds my heart,
That needs but close to press my life away;
Hand in which nature and heaven's self display,
In their own honor, all their craft and art;
Nails, of the rarest pearls the counterpart;   5
Delicate, slender fingers, which today
Naked I've been permitted to survey
(They're not too soft to set my wounds a-smart);
O white and dainty and belovèd glove
In which the ivory and rose has lain,   10
Never was any spoil so sweet as this!
I'll steal as well the veil that hides my love!
No, I'll not steal. Here is your glove again.
—How quick the old woe follows a little bliss!

¹ **gale** in the original *L'aura* with play on *Laura*

CCIV: Sonnet 171

Soul, that such various things with various art
Dost hearken, read, discourse, conceive and write;
Fond eyes, and thou, keen sense framed exquisite
To bear her holy message to the heart:
5 Rejoice ye that it hath not been your part
To gain the road so hard to keep aright
Too late or soon for beacon of her light,
Or guidance her imprinted steps impart.
Now with such beam and such direction blest
10 'Twere shameful in brief way to miss the sign
Pointing the passage to eternal rest.
Upward, faint soul, thy heavenward path incline;
Through clouds of her sweet wrath pursue thy quest,
Following the seemly step and ray divine.

CCV: Sonnet 172

Sweet wrath, sweet scorn, sweet reconcilement, ill
Sweet too, sweet pang, sweet load of tender care,
Sweet tones sped sweetly to enchanted ear,
Sweet balm, sweet fire, alternate to instil—
5 Complain not, soul, but suffer and be still,
Tempering sweet bitterness 'tis thine to bear
With the sweet honour worn in right of her
To whom I said, Thou dost my being fill.
By gentle envy moved, perchance may say
10 Some one in years to come, In his time he
Sore burden for sweet sake of Love hath borne!
Another, Fie on Fortune's cruelty!
How have I missed her? in more recent day
Wherefore not she, or I in earlier born?

CCVIII: SONNET 173 *

Swift river, whom an Alpine fountain feeds,
Who, named from gnawing round thee, go'st thy way,
Craving, along with me by night and day,
Where only Nature thee, but Love me leads!
5 Rush onward! neither weariness impedes,
Nor sleep thy torrent; but before thou pay
The surge his tribute, watch if thou'lt survey
The air more tranquil and more green the meads.
There doth our sweet and living sun appear,
10 Who decks with blossom all thy eastward strand.
Perhaps she thinks me late—what hopes I speak!
Oh kiss her feet, and kiss her fair white hand;
Say kisses must for words be counted here;
The soul is willing, but the flesh is weak.

CCX: SONNET 175

From Spanish Ebro to Hydaspe of Ind,
Though seeking every bay and shore around,
From the Red Sea to cliffs which Caspian bind,
On earth, in heaven is but one Phoenix found.
5 Shall left hand crow or boding raven sound
My fate? My life the Sisters how unwind?
Since ever Pity deaf as asp I find,
And sorrows, where I hoped for joy, abound.
But not in her alone, in him abide
10 Who looks on her, sweet tenderness and love,
So much she has, there flows from her a tide:
And that my sweetness bitterness may prove
Cares not, or caring, sympathy would hide
That Time too soon with grey my hair hath wove.

* Written probably in 1333   ² **gnawing** The Italian for Rhone,
Rodano, suggests the verb *rodere* "to gnaw"

¹ *i.e.* from the Western and Eastern limits of Europe   ⁴ **Phoenix**
see No. clxxxv   ⁵ signs of bad luck   ⁶ **Sisters** the Fates   ⁷ **the**
asp, in order not to hear the enchanter's pipe, was supposed to
press one ear to the ground and cover the other with its tail

CCXI: Sonnet 176

Love guides where spurring Wish would have me sped;
Pleasure plucks on; Use plods with customed feet;
Illusive Hope with kindness counterfeit
Proffers her hand where faint heart beats half dead;
5 This Heart accepts, unwitting we are led
By guides one blindness all, one all deceit;
Sense lords o'er Reason laid in winding-sheet;
And new Desire from old is ever bred.
Virtue and honour, beauty, gracious ways
10 And sweet discourse inveigled to the lime
That snared the silly soul mid lovely treen.
Sixth day of April, at the hour of prime;
Thousand, three hundred, twenty-seven; the maze
I entered whence the issue is not seen.

CCXVII: Sonnet 181

Once I besought her mercy with my sighs,
Striving in love-rime to communicate
My pain, to see in that immaculate
Unmelting heart the fires of pity rise.
5 I longed, the freezing cloud that round her lies
In the eloquent winds of love to dissipate—
Or else I'd rouse against her all men's hate
Because she hid from me her lovely eyes.
But now I wish no longer hate for her,
10 Nor for me, pity; for I know at last
In vain against my fate I spend my breath.
Only I'll sing how she is lovelier
Than the divine, that, when my flesh is cast,
The world may know how happy was my death.

[11] **treen** trees

CCXVIII: Sonnet 182

When among troops of ladies fair and gay
She enters, who on earth hath no compeer,
Befalleth that to them which unto sphere
Of starry night befalls at dawn of day.
Meseems Love standing nigh doth whispering say,   5
"Life shall be comely while she tarrieth here;
Dark and disordered shall it then appear;
And virtues perish, and with them my sway.
As though fell Sun and Moon, from heaven deject,
And air of pulse, and earth of grass and tree,   10
And man were robbed of speech and intellect,
And of all waves and living things the sea;
So pride and joy of life were lorn and wrecked,
If by Death's hand those eyes should veiled be."

CCXIX: Sonnet 183

The songful plaint of birds, newly awake,
Rings through the glimmering vale at morning-tide;
And rills that clear in liquid crystal glide,
With murmuring chimes responsive music make.
And she whose semblance doth of snow partake   5
And gold, grey Tithon's ever-faithful bride,
Cites me with these, o'er heaven disparting wide
The fleecy locks made deathless for her sake.
Thus roused, I Morning greet and Sun in skies,
And Sun more fair wherewith my youth was quelled   10
With daze that hath from then till now endured.
Often together have I marked them rise,
And at encounter of their beams beheld
The stars by him and him by her obscured.

⁶ **Tithon's . . . bride** Aurora, the dawn

CCXXI: Sonnet 185

What destiny of mine, what force, what ruse
Again persuades me weaponless to field
Where always in the shameful dust I yield?
Escape or perish—either way what use?
5 And yet, some use: for through my heart infuse
Such splendours from so sweet, so bright-revealed
A source, the fatal flame still flows that sealed
My doom which now the twentieth year renews.
The couriers of death I feel when those
10 Adorable eyes from dazzling distance come,
And if on me they move as she draws close
With such delicious power Love leaves me numb,
I cannot speak of it, the memory flows
To nothingness; wit, words alike grow dumb!

CCXXII: Sonnet 186

"My strolling ladies, gossiping busily,
Pensive, yet gay; for lack of her, alone;
Your sweet companion, whither is she flown?
Where is my life? Where is the death of me?"
5 "We're gay, because she's quick in memory,
Pensive, because her absence we bemoan;
A jealous heart has marked her for his own,
Raging at thought of her felicity."
"Who can hold lovers so in such oppression?"
10 "Why, the soul's free; but body still must hearken,
As women know, to wrath that domineers;
But often the face transcribes the heart's confession,
And we have seen her stately beauty darken,
And her eyes liquid with a dew of tears."

CCXXIV: Sonnet 188

If cónstancy, a heart that cannot feign,
If sweet-repining honorable desire;
If ardor, burned in chastity of fire;
If the hunt through the labyrinth, in vain;
And if the thoughts writ on the forehead plain   5
But strangled on the lips, when fears conspire
With shame to make them silently retire;
If pallor, violet-tinct with lover's pain;
And if the holding of another dear,
More dear than self; if tears and sighs and woe,   10
Despair and wrath are all one's meat and wine;
If burning far away and freezing near,
Are reasons that in love I suffer so—
Lady, the fault is yours. The hurt is mine.

CCXXVIII: Sonnet 192

My poor heart op'ning with his puissant hand,
Love planted there, as in its home, to dwell
A Laurel, green and bright, whose hues might well
In rivalry with proudest emeralds stand:
Plough'd by my pen and by my heart-sighs fanned,   5
Cooled by the soft rain from mine eyes that fell,
It grew in grace, upbreathing a sweet smell,
Unparalleled in any age or land.
Fair fame, bright honor, virtue firm, rare grace,
The chastest beauty in celestial frame,—   10
These be the roots whence birth so noble came.
Such ever in my mind her form I trace,
A happy burden and a holy thing,
To which on reverent knee with loving prayer I cling.

CCXXXII: Sonnet 196

The victor Alexander wrath defeated,
And made him less a great man than Philippus,
Though, carving him and painting him, Lysippus,
Pyrgoteles, Apelles have competed.
5 By wrath was Tydeus to such madness heated,
That he expired in gnawing Menalippus;
Wrath too made Sylla blind, as well as lippous,
And death at last his punishment completed.
Whereto wrath leadeth, Valentinian knew,
10 And dying Ajax, who less potent came
Against himself, than others to contend.
Wrath's a short madness, but long madness too,
If one refrains it not, and oft to shame
It brings its vassal, sometimes to his end.

CCXXXIV: Sonnet 198

O little room, my harbor from the sea
Of stormy day's tempestuous concerns,
Now all the day's constraining but adjourns
My tears, to spring nocturnally in thee.
5 O little bed, once my security
From grief, upon thee Eros overturns
The gathered pain of tear-collecting urns,
Tilted by two fair hands of ivory.
So now I flee my outraged sanctuary,
10 But most myself, the thoughts of my own mind,
Those very wings whereon I once have flown.
In the hateful, hostile mob (O strange vagary!)
My only port and refuge can I find,
Such is my fear to find myself alone.

[2] **Philippus** Alexander's father   [3-4] **Lysippus** and **Pyrgoteles** were sculptors, **Apelles** a painter; the only artists, it is said, that Alexander permitted to reproduce his likeness   [5-6] **Tydeus** one of the seven against Thebes, who devoured the head of his slain foe, Menalippus   [7] **Sylla** Sulla, dictator of Rome (138-78 B.C.)   [9] **Valentinian** Roman Emperor, died 375 A.D. in an access of rage   [10] **Ajax** slew himself out of anger

CCXL: Sonnet 202 *

Already I have asked Love's intercession
With you, my lady, and I'll ask again
(My bitter joy, and my delicious pain!)
Pardon for my unpardonable transgression.
I'll not deny it, reason and discretion,   5
Which properly the upright soul restrain,
Are impotent when winds of impulse reign
That whirl me into error—and confession.
Your heart, it is so surely comprehending,
And with such heavenly virtue does it brim   10
As never rained from any star in air;
Say then, in undisdainful pity bending:
"What help was there? My face possesses him
Because he is so greedy and I so fair!"

CCXLVI: Sonnet 208

The gentle airs, breathing a little sigh,
Lift the green laurel and her golden hair,
And Laura's face, so delicately fair,
Lets slip my soul to wander far and high.
She is the candid rose, thorn-compassed, shy,   5
And yet our age's glory and despair.
O living Jove, grant me this single prayer,
Grant only that before her death I die.
So I'll not see the sun go out, to bring
The world's disaster, and to leave behind   10
My eyes, no other light discovering,
My soul, to one unending thought confined,
My ears, that never hear another thing
But the sweet language of her modest mind.

* Perhaps composed in 1346

CCXLVIII: Sonnet 210

You seek the best that Nature can confer
Upon our universe? Then come and see
That beauty shining like a sun on me
And on the world, virtue's disparager.
5 Only, come soon; Death ever is astir
To seize the best, leaving the wicked free.
She is too lovely for mortality;
The gods are looking eagerly on her.
Come soon, and you will see all comeliness,
10 All virtue, and all gentle-mannered ways
Sweetly conjoined past any power to sever;
And you will vow my rimes are valueless,
You'll stand so dazzled in delicious maze.
—But if you linger, you will weep forever.

CCXLIX: Sonnet 211 *

I am in terror when I scrutinize
The mind's clear record of our parting day;
I left my heart with her and came away,
And grave and darkly pensive were her eyes.
5 Still like a rose I seem to see her rise
'Mid lovely ladies, lesser flowers were they.
Humbly she stood, nor sorrowful nor gay,
As one whom fear entirely occupies.
Her usual elegance was laid aside,
10 Her pearls and garlands and her colored dress;
She did not laugh and sing and talk again.
And so I left my darling to be tried;
And now black thoughts and dreams and omens press
Hard on my soul; please God it be in vain.

* Written in 1347 or 1348, as likewise it would seem, the two
following sonnets

CCL: SONNET 212

Madonna once would come in dreams to cheer
My slumbers with angelical delight;
But now she brings foreboding in the night,
Nor can I drive away my grief and fear.
And in her phantom-face I see appear   5
Her own hurt mixed with pity for my plight,
And I hear words that cry above my fright
That the final term of joy and hope is near.
"Does our last evening not return to you?"
She says; "Your eyes were wet and shining when   10
For the lateness of the hour I had to flee.
I could not, nor I would not, tell you then,
But now I tell you, it is proved and true;
Never again on earth you'll look on me."

CCLIV: SONNET 216

There is no word of my adorèd one,
My lovely and belovèd enemy,
And frantic hope and fear alternately
Rowel my spirit, on the race they run.
Beauty ere this by beauty's been undone,   5
And she's all beauty and all modesty;
Perhaps God wants such virtuous radiancy
To take from earth, and set in heaven, a sun,
And no mere star. Why then, I'll soon behold
The end of my few joys and many tears.   10
Why did we have to part, that unconsoled
Far from her side, I fill my heart with fears?
The fable of my life will soon be told,
My time is done in the middle of my years.

CCLVI: Sonnet 218

If only time could some revenge obtain me
From her whose every word and glance decried me,
Who then, with sorrier tactics to deride me,
Escapes and veils her eyes, the more to pain me—
5 So cruel—and yet so sweet! Ah, she will drain me,
Exhaust my spirit, tear the soul inside me,
Rage like a lion in my heart to chide me
From sleep and to the clamorous night constrain me!
My soul, expelled from slumber's drowsy dwelling,
10 Left its warm cell and rushed forth disencumbered
To find her who glared menaces unnumbered;
Yet though my soul approached, it baffles telling
That while it talked to her, the blind tears welling,
And clung about her, she lay still and slumbered.

CCLIX: Sonnet 221

I have sought ever ways of solitude,
As brooks and heath and coppice know full well,
Seeking to flee those blunted minds and fell
That would my hope of winning heaven preclude.
5 If I might gain the peace I have pursued,
Since I may not mid Tuscan mountains dwell,
I would abide in Sorga's pleasant dell,
With sighs and lays by its sweet flow renewed.
But I am driven to that place again
10 Where I rage to see my treasure in the dust—
For so wills Fortune, evermore my foe—
Yet to the hand which now enfolds this pen
Fate has for once been kind and mayhap just:
Love witnessed what my Lady and I know.

⁷ *i.e.* in Vaucluse   ⁹ **that place** Avignon   ¹²⁻¹⁴ possibly he means
Laura had clasped his hand in secret

CCLX: Sonnet 222

I've seen a single star of two fair eyes,
Of such a sweet and lofty grace possessed,
That for these dainty bowers, where Love takes rest,
My tired heart must all other sights despise.
Compare not with them that which most you prize   5
In lands or times far distant, not the guest
Whose brilliant beauty once the Greeks distressed
And wrung from Ilion lamentable cries.
Name not Polyxena, Hypsipyle,
Argía, or that fair Roman, who with steel   10
Transfixed her virtuous and indignant heart.
This excellence, if aught aright I feel,
Is Nature's praise, and is delight to me;
But late it came, and ah, must soon depart.

CCLXII: Sonnet 224

"Dear is our life; then virtue doth appear,
Of all fair woman hath, most dear to me."
"Reverse the order, mother; nought can be,
If virtue's absent, either fair or dear.
She that gives up her honour, lingers here   5
Not living and no woman, though you see
Her former semblance; neither is she free
From retributions, more than death, severe.
I have no wonder at Lucretia felt,
Except that grief sufficed her not alone,   10
And that she needed any sword to die."
Oh all ye sages, that herewith have dealt,
Now will a shade upon your tracks be thrown,
And this one teacher will above you fly.

6 guest Helen, "guest" in Troy   **9 Polyxena** slain by Pyrrhus on
the grave of his father, Achilles; **Hypsipyle** queen of Lemnos,
seduced by Jason   **10 Argia** mother of Polynices, executed by
Creon for giving her rebellious son a proper burial; **fair Roman**
is Lucretia, who slew herself after being violated by Tarquin

1-2 are commonly attributed to an older woman, the following
nine to Laura, while the last three contain Petrarch's comment
on the conversation   **9 Lucretia** see cclx

Part II: After Laura's Death

CCLXIV: Ode 21 *

As thought succeeding thought within me springs,
Such keen self-sorrow in my mind is bred
That I am moved to shed
Far other tears than those I wept before;
5 Till, every day drawn nearer to the dead,
From God a thousand times I seek the wings
Whereon to heavenly things
The spirit, freed from earthly bonds, can soar;
Yet strive in vain, for in the end my store
10 Of sighs and tears and prayers must fruitless prove,
And justly so, for if we let our feet
Stumble when we have strength to stand, 'tis meet
We sink, howe'er we long to rise above.
The outstretched arms of Love
15 Are open still, on which my trust is fixed,
And yet I pause perplexed,
Fearful to see my own in others' fate,
A prey to sins I may repent too late.

* Placed by Petrarch at the beginning of the section "In morte di
Laura" this poem nevertheless seems to have been composed
in her lifetime—probably 1348

One thought there is within my mind that pleads:
'What aid supports thee, or what fancy woos?   20
Wretch, seekst thou to excuse
Thy years, which pass but ill for thy repute?
Choose what thy part shall be, and wisely choose:
Subdue thy lusts, tear from thy heart those weeds
Among which nobler seeds   25
Of happiness are strangled ere they shoot.
Tired and contemptuous once, the fond pursuit
Of this world's treacherous and transient gain,
Prized by the rabble, didst thou then give o'er—
Wherefore now are thy longings set once more   30
Where hope of peace or constancy is vain?
While life and strength remain,
And power to curb thy thoughts thou dost not lack,
Let not the rein fall slack:
Well knowst thou there is danger in delay,   35
Nor is repentance sure except today.

'Well knowst thou too already how thy gaze
Long hath surveyed her charms in ecstasy,
Whom I could willingly
Wish, for our greater peace, unborn as yet.   40
Thou canst recall (and shouldst, in verity)
The face whose beauty set thy heart ablaze
When else, perchance, the rays
Of other charms had never kindled it.
But since so long the cheating flame she lit   45
Has burned, while thou didst seek in vain a time
Which, were it come, had only brought thee ill,
Now let a loftier hope direct thy will—
Look where around thee whirls the starry clime,
Unendingly sublime,   50
And if, rejoicing in its torments here,
Thy spirit holds so dear
A passing glance, a word, a song of love,
Think what far greater bliss is found above.'

55 Another thought, which mingles sour and sweet,
Of import glad yet grievous too, doth dwell
Within me, and compel
My heart to lofty hope and passion deep—
Careless, if only fame my story tell,
60 Though ague chill my brow, or feverish heat
In wasted pulses beat.
And since this thought ne'er slain but it will leap
To stronger life, first broke my infant sleep,
It has been growing with me all my days,
65 And in the end we two will share one grave.
But, loosed from flesh, the soul no more need crave
A mortal glory which so soon decays;
Though lettered tribes may praise
A dead man's verse, their words die on the wind.
70 So, lest one day I find
My treasures scattered, henceforth let me clasp
The truth, nor clutch at shades which cheat my grasp.

A third desire thereafter fills my brain,
Shadowed by which no other thought can grow;
75 While seasons come and go,
Heedless of self, for her alone I write.
My heart is softened in the radiant glow
That shines from those fair eyes, and they constrain
My course with such a rein
80 As tricks my cunning and defeats my might.
What matter though my bark be trim and tight,
If, by such cables tied, it be confined
To drift forever in a rock-strewn sea?
O Thou whose grace till now has kept me free
85 From other fetters that enchain mankind,
When wilt Thou put from my mind
The sin and shame wherewith my face is soiled?
Like one in dreams embroiled,
When, fronting death, in haste to arms I stand,
90 An empty scabbard mocks my fumbling hand.

I know myself, nor have I failed to learn
The truth, but I am held in Love's duress,
And farthest they digress
From honour's path who most in him confide;
Nor can I always in my heart repress   95
A noble self-derision, rude and stern,
Until all men discern
Upon my brow the shame I thought to hide.
For, since my heart to mortal things is tied
By faith such as is due to God alone,   100
The better my desires, the worse my shame,
And all the louder conscience shouts my blame
When reason is by appetite o'erthrown.
But though I hear and own
My fault, yet evil habit checks my sighs,   105
Bringing before my eyes
Her form whose birth already rang my knell,
Who pleases both herself and me too well.

What length of years I know not Heaven assigned
When first my feet were set in earthly ways   110
Among these rude affrays
Whose pattern in my own despite I wrought;
Nor to foretell the limit of my days
While yet veiled in flesh avails a mortal mind.
Yet, since my hair is lined   115
With grey, and changed within my every thought,
Feeling that death must surely be my lot
Ere many morrows come, like one made wise
By losses past, I marvel, looking back,
How far my leftward course has left the track   120
On which alone the port of promise lies.
Then shame with sorrow vies
Within to bid me make the leeway good;
But, grown to hardihood,
With age, long as I draw this painful breath,   125
Needs must fond passion bandy terms with Death.

Such then, my song, am I; and at the thought
That I must surely perish, keener cold
Than that of frozen snow invades my heart;
130 For, while I hesitate, the greater part
Of my short web upon the beam is rolled.
Did ever men behold
A heavier weight than that which burdens me?
Death bears me company,
135 Who, seeking counsel for amendment still,
Perceive the good yet choose perforce the ill.

CCLXVII: Sonnet 228 *

Alas, that gentle look, and that fair face!
Alas, for the body's beauty when you wended
Your gracious way! Alas, your words that mended
The wicked, and taught honor to the base!
5 Alas, that smile of yours, whose wounding grace
Has come to death, and all my hope is ended!
You'd have been queen of earth, had you descended
To a younger world, to a less evil race.
Still I must burn in you, in you respire!
10 I was yours utterly; my stricken heart
Can feel no other hurt, after today.
You showered hope upon me and desire
In our last moment, ere we came to part;
And then the wind blew all your words away.

* Apparently written soon after news of Laura's death reached
the poet (in Parma, May 19, 1348—she had died on April 6)

CCLXIX: SONNET 229

Both, broken, lofty column, laurel green,
Whose shade relieved my thought in weary stound!
Lost, what in East or West shall not be found,
Nor India's and Morocco's shores between!
Death hath my double wealth, of which I've been   5
So glad, and have so proudly paced the ground;
For which nor lands nor empire could compound,
Nor piles of gold, nor gems of Morn's demesne.
Yet if to this the Destinies agree,
What can I, but with soul afflicted stay,   10
With ever-moistened eyes and face down-cast?
Alack our life, so beautiful to see,
With how much ease thou losest, in a day,
What many years with pain and toil amassed!

CCLXXI: SONNET 230 *

That fiery snare in which I used to flame,
While for two decades and a year I bore it,
Death has unfastened: never pain before it
Of such intensity touched me, never the same.
But Love, still bent my tortured soul to tame,   5
So spread his net my heart could scarce ignore it,
So fed the fire so trapped my heart and tore it,
That no escape could save me from the shame.
Had I not learned from my first agonies,
I should long since have nourished his fierce hunger—   10
The more so since I shed my innocent green:
Now Death steps forth again to intervene
And split the bond: that blaze flares up no longer
Which neither force nor intellect can appease.

[1] lofty column Cardinal Colonna laurel green Laura; both died in 1348

* We do not know who this second and doomed love of the poet was

CCLXXII: Sonnet 231

Life hurries on, a frantic refugee,
And Death, with great forced marches, follows fast;
And all the present leagues with all the past
And all the future to make war on me.
5 Anticipation joins to memory
To search my soul with daggers; and at last,
Did not damnation set me so aghast,
I'd put an end to thinking, and be free.
The few glad moments that my heart has known
10 Return to me; then I foresee in dread
The winds upgathering against my ways,
Storm in the harbor, and the pilot prone,
The mast and rigging down; and dark and dead
The lovely lights whereon I used to gaze.

CCLXXIII: Sonnet 232

What are you doing? Why do you backward peer
Still at the days that vanished long ago,
My soul, disconsolate? Why do you throw
Wood on the fire that burns you, flaming clear?
5 All her soft words and gentle glances dear
Which you have limned and celebrated so,
Are reft from earth away. And well you know
It is too late. You will not find them here.
Rouse not again that sleeping agony,
10 Follow no more those thoughts that lead astray,
Take the sure road; our only heed shall be
Heaven; there's naught on earth to make us stay.
Oh all that beauty was calamity,
If living or dead it takes our peace away!

CCLXXIV: Sonnet 233

O unforgiving thoughts, I pray you: Peace!
Must I contend with Love and Death and Fate
Hot at the walls and pressing at the gate
Whilst inward rebels give me no surcease?
Ah, heart of mine, what treacherous caprice   5
Has made of you a cruel confederate
With every eager foeman of my state?
'Tis through your faithlessness my woes increase.
All secret messages of Love you know;
Fortune displays its every pomp to you;   10
Death shares with you the memory of that blow
Which must these sad remains of me undo,
You give false arms to each fond thought, and so
Yours is the blame for every grief I rue.

CCLXXIX: Sonnet 238 *

If I do hear regretful birds complain
—Or the leaves ruffling in the summer light,
Or water whispering huskily toward the plain—
From my resort, where streamside flowers are bright,
And where I sit, and dream of love, and write;   5
Then do I see and hear her once again
Whom heaven vouchsafed a moment to our sight;
Her far voice comes in answer to my pain:
"Why do you waste away in such advance
Of time? And why—" so, gently, does she chide,   10
"Do you walk always in a tearful trance?
Weep not for me; out of the death I died
I rose immortal; and in radiance
My eyes, that seemed to shut, have opened wide."

* Written during the poet's last sojourn in Vaucluse, 1351-3,
as also the following sonnet

CCLXXXI: Sonnet 240

How often, to my dear retreat, in flight
From all men, from my own self most of all,
I come, to breathe upon the air my plight,
And let my tears incessantly down fall!
5 How often, solitary, touched with fright,
Under the grim and shadowy forest pall
I go to dream again the high delight
Which Death has taken! And answering my call,
Now like a river nymph in silver showers
10 Of Sorgue's bright waters does she rise; I see
Her calmly sitting in the streamside bowers
Or treading the young grass composedly,
Stirring, like any living soul, the flowers;
Her face revealing that she pities me.

CCLXXXVII: Sonnet 246 *

Friend Sennuccio! though mournful and alone,
Thou leavest me, I yet am comforted,
Since from the prison that held thee bound and dead,
Scorning, thou hast to life and freedom flown.
5 Now both the poles by thee are seen and known,
And how the pilgrim stars 'cross heaven are led,
Thou seest, and how our sight is limited,
So from the bliss my grief has milder grown.
But greet in yon third sphere good Master Cino,
10 Guittone, Dante, and the brotherhood,
That throngs around them, and our loved Franceschino.
And to my lady too sure tidings bring,
How I live sadly in wild solitude,
Her beauty and pure life remembering.

* Sennuccio died in the autumn of 1349; see cxii
⁹ **third sphere** that of Venus; see xxxi **Cino** see xcii   ¹⁰ **Guittone**
Guittone d'Arezzo, fore-runner of Dante, died 1294   ¹¹ **Fran-
ceschino** Francesco degli Albizzi, minor poet and intimate of
Petrarch, died of the plague in the spring of 1348

CCXC: Sonnet 249

So goes the world! That now affords delight
Which once most sorely grieved me. Now 'tis plain
That safety may be only won by pain,
And peace eternal after stress of fight,
Hopes and desires deceitful to the sight,   5
Falser a hundredfold in lovers' brain!
Had she who leaves her grave in heaven to reign
Yielded me grace—what then had been my plight!
Blind love and a deaf mind had made me stray
So far abroad that in the search for life   10
Needs through death's confines I must travel still.
Blessèd be she who taught the better way,
And checked with gentle hand, 'mid ardent strife,
So that I perish not, my headstrong will!

CCXCII: Sonnet 251 *

Those eyes in which I used to put my trust,
Those arms and hands and feet that would beguile
My spirit from its fleshly domicile,
Far from the homely world of man out-thrust;
That crisping gleaming golden hair; the gust   5
Of angel-laughter heard behind her smile
That used to make earth paradise awhile;
These are now dust in the unfeeling dust.
And yet I live and breathe! I know not why!
Life fills me all with self-reproach and scorning.   10
No shore-light guides my bark; the storm is high.
I'll sing of love no more. The needless warning
Comes when my wonted vein is sear and dry.
My harp, it shall be turned alone to mourning.

* Perhaps written in 1357

CCXCIII: Sonnet 252

Had I but known the world would so much care
To hear my utterances of grief in rhyme,
Then had I made them from the earliest time
In count more copious, in style more rare.
5 She for whom erst my sighs did fill the air
In homage of her qualities sublime
Is dead now and my muse no more may climb
Above the harsh and rough notes of despair.
I sang of old in hope but of relieving
10 My heavy burden, trusting thereby merely
To ease my heart; for fame was ne'er my spur.
Solace I sought, not glory in my grieving;
Now would I please indeed, but she austerely
In silence summons me to follow her.

CCXCVI: Sonnet 255

Wonted to self-reproach, I now excuse
Myself, nay laud, and rate my worth the more
For honour of captivity I bore,
And sweet sad wound long hid in heart secluse:
5 And rather the invidious Fates accuse
Who marred the spindle whence the chain I wore
Devolved so fair, and broke Love's arrow, sore,
But gilt with loveliness past mortal use.
For never in her days was soul so fain
10 Of liberty and joy and life's glad lot,
But would its natural wish for her deny;
Preferring rather for her sake to plain
Than sing for others; prisoned in such knot
Content to live, pierced with such wound to die.

CCCI: Sonnet 260 *

Valley, my sorrow's refuge and retreat;
River, whereto my tears are tributary;
Wild birds and beasts; and fishes, shy and wary,
Within the green walls of your narrow street;
Air, that receives and soothes my passion's heat;   5
Pathway of grief, where once I was so merry;
Hill, joyful once, and now pain's sanctuary,
Whither Love still compels my docile feet;
Your dear familiar forms I recognize,
But not myself; I am no longer gay,   10
I am an inn for everlasting dole.
Here, where we walked, I see her spirit rise,
Naked and pure, to take the heavenly way,
Leaving on earth the garments of her soul.

CCCII: Sonnet 261

In thought I raised me to the place where she
Whom still on earth I seek and find not, shines;
There 'mid the souls whom the third sphere confines,
More fair I found her and less proud to me.
She took my hand and said: Here shalt thou be   5
With me ensphered, unless desires mislead;
Lo! I am she who made thy bosom bleed,
Whose day ere eve was ended utterly:
My bliss no mortal heart can understand;
Thee only do I lack, and that which thou   10
So loved, now left on earth, my beauteous veil.
Ah! wherefore did she cease and loose my hand?
For at the sound of that celestial tale
I all but stayed in Paradise till now.

* Also of the 1351-3 period

⁸ **third sphere** See xxxi

CCCIV: Sonnet 263

While on my heart the worms consuming prey'd
Of Love, and I with all his fire was caught;
The steps of my fair wild one still I sought
To trace o'er desert mountains as she stray'd;
5 And much I dared in bitter strains to upbraid
Both Love and her, whom I so cruel thought;
But rude was then my genius, and untaught
My rhymes, while weak and new the ideas play'd.
Dead is that fire; and cold its ashes lie
10 In one small tomb; which had it still grown on
E'en to old age, as oft by others felt,
Arm'd with the power of rhyme, which wretched I
E'en now disclaim, my riper strains had won
E'en stones to burst, and in soft sorrows melt.

CCCX: Sonnet 269 *

Zephyr returns, and scatters everywhere
New flowers and grass, and company does bring,
Procne and Philomel, in sweet despair,
And all the tender colors of the Spring.
5 Never were fields so glad, nor skies so fair;
And Jove exults in Venus' prospering.
Love is in all the water, earth, and air,
And love possesses every living thing.
But to me only heavy sighs return
10 For her who carried in her little hand
My heart's key to her heavenly sojourn.
The birds sing loud above the flowering land;
Ladies are gracious now.—Where deserts burn
The beasts still prowl on the ungreening sand.

* Written probably in 1352; so too the following sonnet
¹ **Zephyr** the west wind of spring ³ **Procne and Philomel** Greek
figures of the old legend, turned respectively into swallow and
nightingale

CCCXI: SONNET 270

Yon nightingale whose melancholy trill,
Perhaps in longing for his missing mate,
Soars heavenward above the plain and hill,
Fills the deep night with sweetness desolate.
Through the dark hours I hear him singing still,   5
Seeming to mourn with me my sorry fate
Who once had fondly thought Death's regal will
Could not prevail 'gainst goddesses' estate.
How Fortune brings to earth the oversure!
Those lights that once, alas, as brightly burned   10
As any sun are quenched now and obscure.
No more for me fair prospect may allure;
Henceforth I live as one who well has learned
How nothing that here pleases can endure.

CCCXII: SONNET 271

Nor spangled stars, unclouded skies among,
Nor ships that glide sunlit o'er tranquil seas,
Nor deer seen gaily leaping through the trees,
Nor lancers 'midst the plains in glittering throng,
Nor fresh-brought news of good, expected long,   5
Nor lofty rhymes of love which flow with ease,
Nor 'midst clear streams, in arbours fanned by breeze,
Fair noble ladies singing some sweet song,
Nor aught of joy, can reach my heart, which lies
Buried with her, who took it to the grave,   10
The only light and mirror of my eyes.
Life is such deep disgust, and has long been,
That now I beg the end, I so much crave
To see her, whom I had best never seen.

CCCXV: Sonnet 274 *

All my green years and golden prime of man
Had pass'd away, and with attemper'd sighs
My bosom heaved—ere yet the days arise
When life declines, contracting its brief span.
5 Already my loved enemy began
To lull suspicion, and in sportive guise,
With timid confidence, though playful, wise,
In gentle mockery my long pains to scan:
The hour was near when Love, at length, may mate
10 With Chastity; and, by the dear one's side,
The lover's thoughts and words may freely flow:
Death saw, with envy, my too happy state,
E'en its fair promise—and, with fatal pride,
Strode in the midway forth, an armed foe!

CCCXVI: Sonnet 275

Some peace, some armistice we might have made
To end our warring—but then on the scene
Broke the Great Leveller to intervene
And all our virtuous hopes were straight betrayed.
5 Even as the mists before the wind must fade
So she who was my heart's delight, my queen,
Has fled away and presently I mean
To leave the world and follow her sweet shade.
But yet a little and the turning seasons
10 And greying looks would soon have spent our fire
And *sans* reproach we might have talked of love.
How chastely then—it was my fond desire—
I would have told my passion and its reasons,
Which now she knows and pities from above.

* This and the following sonnet were written probably in the Autumn of 1351 or early 1352

CCCXVIII: Sonnet 277

Where late one tree, as if by tempest's play,
Or smitten by the axe, had met its fall,
Bringing to earth its glorious spoils withal,
And its blanched roots exposing to the day,
I saw another, object of Love's sway,   5
My constant subject at the muses' call,
Which as the ivy clings to tree or wall
Will with the heart it fettered ever stay.
That living laurel (where in tender nest
My best thoughts harboured and the burning sighs   10
Powerless on those fair boughs to stir a leaf)
To heaven translated, in this faithful breast
Hath left its roots, so still there's one who cries
Although none answer to the tones of grief.

CCCXIX: Sonnet 278

O swifter than the fawn my days have fled,
A dream of shadows; one look, wild, misleading,
Sums up my whole delight: come, end the reading,
With little sweet, with bitter surfeited!
O wretched world, of doubt and darkness bred,   5
Who trusts in thee is lost! My love, my pleading,
My hopes were thine: all dead with my heart bleeding,
With her heart dust among the indifferent dead!
The flesh outmoded, still she burns, and still
In her high heaven, a bright and deathless flower,   10
Infects me with her flame, hour after hour.
So, though I whiten momently, my will
Increases, brooding on her house, her doom,
The lovely flesh she never will resume.

CCCXXI: Sonnet 280 *

Is this the nest wherein my Phoenix laid
The purple of her plumage and the gold,
Whose sheltering pinions did my heart enfold,
That still to sigh and song she doth persuade?
5 Source of my sweetest ill, where now displayed
The countenance whence leapt the light of old
That in consuming kept me glad and bold?
Earth's star thou wert, now star of Heaven art made.
Unmated now, save with my miseries,
10 I bear my burden back unto the place
That for her sake who hallowed it I prize:
Viewing obscurity the hills efface
Where thy regard made splendour for a space,
And thy last flight was taken to the skies.

CCCXXVII: Sonnet 283

The ardour and the odour and dark wonder
Of my sweet laurel and her golden glamour
That offered quiet from the dusty clamour,
Death the Despoiler tramples down in thunder.
5 As when the moon presses the proud sun under,
So now my lights go out, my voices stammer;
On Death I cry to halt Death's heavy hammer—
With such black thoughts Love tears my heart asunder.
O lovely lady, brief the sleep you slumbered:
10 An instant only, then amid the numbered
You woke to gaze with them on God's deep glory:
And if my verse its cunning still recovers,
Among the noble minds, the noble lovers
It shall record your name, your deathless story.

* Perhaps also written in 1351

CCCXXXII: Sestina 9 *

My fortune once so kind, my life so blithe,
My days of sunshine, and my tranquil nights,
And my sweet sighs, and that delightsome style
Which hath made tunable my verse and rhymes,
These all, turned suddenly to grief and tears,   5
Make me now hate my life and long for death.

Oh cruel, keen, inexorable Death,
Thou causest that I never can be blithe,
But utterly must waste my life in tears,
My days in darkness, and in woe my nights.   10
My deep-drawn sighs can find no place in rhymes,
And my sharp anguish baffles every style.

Whereunto hath been drawn my amorous style?
To speak of anger, and discourse of death.
Whereto have come the verses and the rhymes   15
To which a gracious heart has harkened blithe?
Where is my utterance of love by nights,
When now I think and talk of only tears?

So sweet my passion rendered once my tears,
That dainty they could make a rugged style,   20
And waking have they kept me livelong nights.
Now is my weeping bitter more than death,
For I've no hope of those fair glances blithe
Which gave high matter to my lowly rhymes.

Love had his fair mark set before my rhymes   25
Within those eyes, now sets it in my tears,
Recalling to me sadly moments blithe.
So with my thoughts I alter now my style,
And I begin to entreat of thee, pale Death,
That thou'lt withdraw me from such grievous nights.   30

* Probably composed in 1359 or 1360

Slumber it fled from my tormented nights,
And wonted cadence from my croaking rhymes,
Which can discourse of nothing now but death;
And all my singing hath been turned to tears.
35 Love in his realm hath no such varied style,
That is so mournful, and hath been so blithe.

Of all men living I was once most blithe;
Now is there none so sad by days and nights;
And with my grief grows heavier my style,
40 My heart dictating lamentable rhymes.
I lived in hope, and now I live in tears,
And trust no remedy, but death, for death.

Death's for me done his worst, and only Death
Can make me meet again that aspect blithe
45 That made me feel a joy in sighs and tears,
The pleasant airs and showers of my nights,
Wile I was weaving choicer thoughts in rhymes,
And Love would elevate my feeble style.

Now would to heav'n I'd such a melting style,
50 That I could win my Laura back from death,
As Orpheus did his love, though not by rhymes,
For then should I live more than ever blithe.
If that's past hope, may one among these nights
For ever close the fountains of my tears.

55 These many, many years, oh Love, with tears
I've conned my grievous loss in rueful style,
Nor dost thou give me hope of easier nights.
Therefore have I been moved to pray for Death,
That he may take me hence to make me blithe,
60 Where she is, whom I sing and mourn in rhymes.

If to such height could soar my feeble rhymes
As her to reach, who rose past wrath and tears,
And with her beauties now makes heaven blithe,
Well might she recognise my altered style,
Which pleased her once perhaps, before yet Death 65
Had brought her cloudless days and me black nights.

Oh ye, that sigh to have more happy nights,
And ye, that hear or tell of Love in rhymes,
Pray, that a favour I may win from Death,
That port of sorrows, and that end of tears. 70
Oh let him change for once his wonted style,
Which makes all sad; for he can make me blithe,

Can make me blithe in one or some few nights,
In rugged style, and in these painful rhymes,
I pray now Death, that he may end my tears. 75

CCCXXXIII: SONNET 287

Go, grieving verses, to yon cruel stone
Whereunder my most cherished treasure lies—
Nay, rather bid her listen from the skies;
Earth holds not her but flesh and lifeless bone.
Tell her how weary all my days have grown, 5
How my poor foundering bark forlornly plies
The troubled seas; how I still save and prize
The scattered leaves of memory—alone.
Only of her they speak, in life or death—
Nay, never dead but living and immortal, 10
And to the whole wide world they make her dear;
So may it please her at my life's last breath
To greet me at the Heavenly City's portal
In her new loveliness. The hour draws near.

CCCXXXVI: Sonnet 290

Undimmed, unfading in my mind is she,
Returning o'er oblivious Lethe's bed,
Seeming again a radiance to shed
As in her flowery age, unceasingly.
5 And so demurely beautiful I see
Her feature, that I cry, bewilderèd;
"It is her very self! She is not dead!"
And clamor to her that she speak to me.
Now she replies; now she is obdurate;
10 I catch at reason, lost a little time,
And make the mind repeat the truth it knows:
'Twas the year thirteen hundred forty-eight,
The sixth of April, in the hour of prime,
That from the body that dear soul arose.

CCCXXXVII: Sonnet 291

That which in perfume and in lustre vied
With the translucent odorous Orient—
Fruits, flowers, herbs and leaves of every scent—
Through whom the West obtained the wreath of pride:
5 My lovely laurel which has deified
All grace, all beauty, virtue's tower and tent,
Lo, underneath its shadowy firmament
God and my Goddess sitting side by side!
Still in that cherished plant have I reposed
10 My worthiest of thoughts: in fire, in frost,
Trembling or burning, still have I been blest.
And when the flame fell, when the chapter closed,
The world filled with her to the uttermost—
God raised her up and took her to His Breast.

CCCXL: Sonnet 294

Dear precious pledge, by Nature snatch'd away,
But yet reserved for me in realms undying;
O thou on whom my life is aye relying,
Why tarry thus, when for thine aid I pray?
Time was, when sleep could to mine eyes convey   5
Sweet visions, worthy thee;—why is my sighing
Unheeded now?—who keeps thee from replying?
Surely contempt in heaven cannot stay:
Often on earth the gentlest heart is fain
To feed and banquet on another's woe   10
(Thus love is conquer'd in his own domain),
But thou, who seest through me, and dost know
All that I feel,—thou, who canst soothe my pain,
Oh! let thy blessèd shade its peace bestow.

CCCXLI: Sonnet 295

Kind Heaven, what angel messenger was wrought
So swift with my complaint on high to speed?
For now my Love returns in very deed,
As erst with comeliness and sweetness fraught;
And balsam for the wretched heart hath brought,   5
Humbly attending on her holy deed;
And such, in fine, that I from death recede,
And live, nor sorrow for the life resought.
O fortunate, that can another bless
By the mere sight, or words that softly thrill   10
But in his ear who knows what they express!
"Dear faithful friend, I sorrow for thy ill,
But I was cruel for our happiness."
Thus she, and more to make the sun stand still.

CCCXLVI: Sonnet 300

The flower of angels and the spirits blest,
Burghers of heaven, on that first day when she
Who is my lady died, around her pressed
Fulfilled with wonder and with piety.
5 What light is this? What beauty manifest?
Marvelling they cried: for such supremacy
Of splendor in this age to our high rest
Hath never soared from earth's obscurity.
She, glad to have exchanged her spirit's place,
10 Consorts with those whose virtues most exceed;
At times the while she backward turns her face
To see me follow—seems to wait and plead:
Therefore toward heaven my will and soul I raise,
Because I hear her praying me to speed.

CCCXLVII: Sonnet 301

Lady! thou 'rt happy with thy Maker now,
Since thy pure life has earned its guerdon meet,
Raised to that glorious and lofty seat,
In richer sheen than pearls and gold bestow;
5 'Mong other Ladies high and rare art thou:
In sight of Him who seeth all, repeat
The story of my love, faith pure and sweet,
Which caused my tears and all my rhymes to flow.
Thou know'st my heart on earth was always thine,
10 As now it is in heaven; nor ever turned,
But to regard the sunshine of thine eyes;
Hence to repay the strife that long was mine,
In seeking thee, when all things else I spurned,
I pray that to thy presence soon I rise.

CCCXLIX: Sonnet 303 *

From hour to hour I seem to hear her calling—
My Lady calling! Gladly would I answer!
I feel decay within me like a cancer;
And am so changed—with more than gray years crawl-
    ing—
Mine own eyes find me foreign and appalling   5
Like some old ghost, some withered necromancer;
How long must I pipe on or play the dancer
In this unholy jest with phantoms brawling?
O day of my deliverance when this prison
Shall split, the rock burst and I stand up-risen,   10
Shedding this flesh so onerous and frail!
When from this dungeon night my soul sets sail,
An eagle cleaving leagues of wind and weather
To where my Lord and Lady walk together!

CCCLIII: Sonnet 307

O lovely little bird, I watch you fly,
And grieving for the past I hear you sing,
Seeing the night and winter hastening,
Seeing the day and happy summer die.
If you could hear my heart in answer cry   5
Its pain to your sad tune, you'd swiftly wing
Into my bosom, comfort you would bring,
And we would weep together, you and I.
'Tis no equality of woe, I fear;
Perhaps she lives whom you bewail; from me   10
Have greedy death and heaven snatched my dear.
But the dark autumn evening hour sets free
The memory of many a banished year;
So let us talk of the past then, tenderly.

* Perhaps another of the 1351-3 period

CCCLVIII: Sonnet 312

Death cannot sour the sweetness of her face,
Her sweet face can the sour of death dispel;
She taught me the good life, and now she shall
Teach me to die the good death, in its place.
5   And He who shed His blood to give us grace,
Who with His foot broke ope the gates of hell,
Comforts me by His blessèd death, as well.
So come, dear Death; come, with thy kind embrace.
And it is time, O Death, do not delay;
10   It was high time after thy cruel power
Had made Madonna from the world ascend.
We'd walked together all along the way;
Together did we come to the utmost hour;
And where she halted is my journey's end.

CCCLXIV: Sonnet 316

Through twenty-one long years Love held me burning
In blissful flame whilst hope assuaged the smart;
My lady, bearing Heavenward my heart,
Left me another ten in fruitless yearning.
5   A-weary now, in my life's course discerning
How wayward error, with persistent art,
Has smothered virtue, ere I yet depart,
To Thee, All Highest, all my vows are turning.
Sad and remorseful for the years thus spent,
10   Years that I should have put to better use,
In fleeing ill, in seeking true content,
Lord, I implore Thee, from this prison loose
My soul; withheld eternal banishment:
I know my sin and offer no excuse.

[5-7] Suggest the poem commemorates an Easter Sunday—it is not certain of what year

[1-4] indicate the poem was written in 1358, probably on or close to April 6; the following sonnet is of the same period

CCCLXV: Sonnet 317

How I go grieving for the days on earth
I passed in worship of a mortal thing,
Heedless to fledge the spiritual wing,
Careless, to try the measure of my worth.
Thou who dost know my every sin from birth,   5
Invisible, immortal, heavenly king,
Help thou my soul, so weak and wandering,
Pour thy abundant grace upon its dearth.
Out of the battle, out of the hurricane,
I come to harbor; may my passing be   10
Worthy, as all my dwelling here was vain;
And may Thy hand be quick to comfort me
In death, and in the hours that still remain.
Thou knowest, I have no other hope but Thee.

CCCLXVI: Ode 29

Virgin most fair, who, clad and crown'd with sun
   And stars, didst please the Sun supreme so well,
     That for His light He made a tent in thee,
   Love bids me something of thy praises tell,
But nought, without thy aid, can be begun,   5
     And His, who loved thy body's guest to be.
     I cry to one, who answers graciously
Whoe'er in faith implore.
If ever yet the sore
     Sufferings of man have touch'd thy clemency,   10
Virgin, oh now to my petition lean;
     Do thou my warfare aid,
Though I be made of earth, and thou heaven's queen.

Virgin most wise, and numbered in that band
15   Of virgins that are blessed and discreet!
        Yea, first thereof, and with the clearest light—
    Thou trusty shield, when Death and Fortune beat
Poor wretches down, that canst all blows withstand,
      Assuring us of triumph, not retreat;
20   Relief of troubled hearts from that wild heat
Which here men's follies raise—
Oh Virgin, let the gaze
    Of those fair eyes, which did in sorrow meet
On thy sweet Son's dear limbs each ghastly trace,
      Be turned to my distress,
Who, succourless, for succour seek thy face.

Virgin most pure, in whom no blemish lies,
    Daughter and mother of thy birth divine,
      Light of this life, of yonder life the grace,
30 Thou bright and lofty window of the skies,
    By thee our most high Father's child and thine
      Came down to save the latest of our race;
      And amid every mortal dwelling-place,
Thou, saintly maid, alone
35 Wast chosen, that the moan
    Of Eve thou shouldst with jubilee replace.
Oh make me, for thou canst, His grace beseem,
    Thou that beyond all bound
Art blest, and crowned in yonder court supreme.

Virgin most holy, full of grace, that wast   40
  Exalted by thy deep, true humbleness
    To heav'n, whence thou my orison dost hear;
  Thou broughtest forth the Fount of tenderness
And Sun of justice, who the world, when lost
    In errors dense and dark, made bright and clear.   45
    Three names thou linkest, that are sweet and dear—
Mother, and child, and bride.
Oh Virgin glorified
  Queen of that Lord, who to this earthly sphere,
Loosing our bonds, brought liberty with bliss;   50
    True Comforter, impart
Peace to my heart by those blest wounds of His.

Virgin, apart from all and singly placed,
  Who with thy beauties hast enamoured Heav'n,
    Whom none precedeth, none hath seconded;   55
  Thou that to God hast veritably given,
By holy thoughts and acts devout and chaste,
    A temple in thy fruitful maidenhead;
    By thee my life to gladness can be led,
If by my prayer, kind maid,   60
Sweet Mary, thou be sway'd,
    Where sin abounds, that grace as far may spread.
Lo, on my spirit's bended knees I pray,
    That, tow'rd a better end,
Thou may'st amend my misdirected way.   65

Bright Virgin, that for ever dost abide,
   Thou lodestar on this ocean tempest-vex'd,
    Thou trusted guide of every seaman true,
   Look, with how dire a storm I stand perplexed,
70 Helmless, without one helper at my side,
     How close on me the pangs of death pursue.
     But thou my soul's hope art; to thee I sue,
  While sinful granting it—
  Virgin, do not permit
75   Thy foe to boast that he can make me rue.
Remember, that God even for our sin,
    To rescue us from doom,
Did flesh assume, thy virgin shrine within.

Virgin, how many tears have I now spent,
80   With many a blandishment and many a vow,
   All to my hurt and my incumbrance sore.
  Since I was born in Arno's vale till now,
By turns to this and that direction bent,
   My life has been but trouble evermore.
85   Of mortal charms, words, graces, what a store
Hath cumbered all my mind!
O Virgin holy and kind,
   Delay not, for my last year I may score.
As swift as arrows fly, my days have flown
90   In wretchedness and sin;
And I begin to wait for death alone.

Virgin, thou know'st who moulders, and my heart
  Leaves wretched, which she kept in languishment;
    And where a thousand things were wrong, not one
  I knew; yet had I known them all, the event   95
Were equal—had she played a different part,
    Her fame, and my salvation were undone.
    O queen of heav'n, our Goddess, if I run
Into no terms forbid—
Thou, from whom nought is hid,   100
    Deep-scanning Virgin, things as yet by none
Performed, are nought to thy great potency.
    Now therefore end my woe,
Reap honour so thyself, and save thou me.

Virgin, on whom alone my hopes relie,   105
  Who canst and wilt to my sore trouble give
    Thy succours, be thou with me to my end.
  Regard not me, but by whose grace I live;
Let not my merit, but that image high
    Which in me dwells, a man so mean commend.   110
    Thou see'st me like a rock, from which descend,
O Virgin, idle streams;
Some Gorgon or my dreams
    Have shaped me thus; but sorrows do thou send
More soft and holy to this breast outworn.   115
    Make my last tears devout
And pure throughout, though some were madness-born.

[92] who Laura

Virgin humane, pride's foe, if dear thou hold
  The common prototype of thee and us,
120   Have pity upon my humbled heart contrite.
  For, if I loved, with faith so marvellous,
A piece of earth, a brittle mortal mould,
      Thou, noblest thing, may'st more my zeal incite.
      If then from my debased and wretched plight
125 Thy hand uplifteth me,
Virgin, I pledge to thee
      My chastened pen, my thoughts, my inmost might,
My tongue, my heart, and every tear and sigh;
      O let my changed desire
130 Thy grace acquire; guide me where true fords lie.

My hour is toward—far it cannot lurk;
  Time runs and flies so well,
  Oh Virgin nonpareil,
While on my heart both Death and Conscience work.
135 Commend me to thy Son, for God indeed
  And Man indeed is He,
That peacefully my last breath He may speed.

METRICAL LETTERS

To Giacomo Colonna *

Yet even here she comes, claiming her rights:
Waking, I still behold her; and her brow
Brings terror even to my fitful sleep.
Often, O wonder! in the dead of night,
Passing my thrice-barred door, she seeks me out,   5
Sure of my slavery: I cannot move,
And suddenly through all my veins my blood
Gathers to guard the citadel of my heart.
If one should enter with a lantern then,
And see me where I lie, he would behold   10
My face pale with the fear that fills my breast.
I wake in tears, rise from my bed, and swiftly,
Before the white bride of Tithonus brings
Her light to the horizon, leaving my house—
My house of fear—I seek the woods and the hills,   15
Casting my glance around, lest she, pursuing,
Prevent my wandering steps. Nay—past belief
Though it may be, and truly as I hope
For surcease from this torment—when I think
To be alone in pathless forest shades,   20
I see the face I fear, upon the bushes
Or on an oaken trunk; or from the stream
She rises; flashes on me from a cloud
Or from clear sky; or issues from a rock,
Compelling me, dismayed, to hold my step.   25

* Ep. Met. I, 6, written in 1338. Only the second part of this
rather long letter appears here
[1] she Laura   [13] bride of Tithonus Aurora, the dawn

123

Such snares Love spreads for me, nor have I hope
Save in the mercy of almighty God,
That from this tempest He may rescue me,
Defeat the wiles of the enemy, and permit
30 Me to live safe within this hiding place.
     Enough of this—but you would still have more.
Hear then the story of my common days.
     Light is my evening meal, seasoned with hunger
And with the toil and fasting of the day.
35 Companions have I none, save only three:
My faithful dog, my servants, and myself.
All others, fearful, shun this spot, wherefrom
Pleasure, though armed with arrows of desire,
Takes flight to find her place in city wealth.
40 The Muses, from their exile now released,
Share my retreat, but visitors are few,
Save those who come to see the famous Fountain.
'Tis much if once or twice within the year
Old friends of mine enter this Vale Enclosed:
45 Distance o'ercomes affection. But their letters
Visit me constantly, and breathe my name
In winter evenings by the glowing hearth
Or in the coolness of the summer shade:
Ever by day and night they speak of me.
50 Yet friends are absent, for they dread the thorns
And the snows that here surround me, and my food
Is hard to those who feed on softer fare.
Comrades have failed me, servants drift away
From this austerity I now profess;
55 And if one comes old friendship to renew
He pities me as though I were in prison,
And soon makes his escape. The country folk
Marvel that I despise those rare delights
That seem to them supreme. They do not know
60 My joy: my company of secret friends.
     They come to me from every century
And every land, illustrious in speech,

⁴⁴ **Vale Enclosed** Vaucluse

In mind, and in the arts of war and peace.
Only a corner in my house they ask;
They heed my every summons: at my call   65
They are with me, ever welcome while they stay,
Ready to go, if I wish, and to return.
Now these, now those I question, and they answer
Abundantly. Sometimes they sing for me;
Some tell me of the mysteries of nature;   70
Some give me counsel for my life and death;
Some tell of high emprise, bringing to mind
Ages long past; some with their jesting words
Dispel my sadness, and I smile again;
Some teach me to endure, to have no longing,   75
To know myself. Masters are they of peace,
Of war, of tillage, and of eloquence,
And travel o'er the sea. When I am bowed
With sorrow, they restore me; when I meet
With Fortune's favor, they restrain my pride,   80
Reminding me that the days of life are fleeting.
So much they give: they ask but for a home.
They too have known adversity; and few
And hesitant are those that give them refuge.
The humblest shelter is to them a mansion   85
Where, trembling, they may linger, till the clouds
Are gone, and till the Muses rule again.
They ask no silken hangings on my walls,
No rich and steaming foods upon my board,
No echoing hall resounding with the noise   90
Of those who serve a throng of banqueters.
They gather in contentment: what they have
They give me, as I sit upon my bench
Of rosy wood, in weariness and hunger.
They comfort me, refreshing me with food   95
That has the sacred power to revive,
And drink that is as nectar for its sweetness.
    Even afield they come with me, through groves
And meadows dear to the Nymphs; with me they hate
The common chatter, and the city's tumult.   100
Whole days we spend alone, in lonely woods.

My pen in my right hand, and in my left
My paper, cares and thoughts filling my heart,
We wander on. At times we find ourselves
105 Close to the den of some wild beast, or else
Follow the ceaseless singing of a bird.
Then am I grieved if any come that way
Upon the shady path, and give me greeting—
My thought being intent on higher things.
110 So then I breathe the silence of the forest:
No sound is welcome, save it be the rippling
Of a clear stream upon the sands, or wind
Fluttering my papers, till the songs thereon
Murmur in gentle answer. Oftentimes
115 We linger till my lengthening shadow warns
Of coming night, or night already come
Bids us to speed return—and Vesper then
Lights us upon our path amid the brambles,
Or Dian, rising after the Sun has set.
120   Such then am I, such is the life I lead.
If the one torment that besets me still
Could end at last, then would I call myself
Happy, and born under a kindly star.

TO CARDINAL GIOVANNI COLONNA[*]

Most things grow less with time: your gifts to me
Increase as time goes on, and in my use
They gain in value. So this dog of yours—
Brought to you from the west, accustomed once
To a royal mansion and to royal food   5
And to proud sleep upon a purple bed—
Quickly forgetting his paternal ways,
His Spanish palaces and sleep and food,
Prefers this hard Romulian fare of mine;
And seeing all things new, and thinking them   10
Better than ever, with his simple lot
Is well content.
          When I had come to you
To take my leave, you gave him, so you said,
To be a cheery comrade on my way;
And he, brought down from high to low estate,   15
Obeyed, and sadly let me put a chain
Upon his neck, and followed me. And now
He does the bidding of his humbler master,
And bit by bit forgets the luxuries
He has left behind. He likes to roam the fields;   20
And swimming the clear streams he bites the water
And plays in the pure pools. He likes my food,
My life of leisure, my relief from cares.
No more does he regret the ample halls
And the varied dainties of his former lord: 25
This food and water and this little house
Suffice for him. His body, washed in the stream,
Is shining now. He is free at last of the mange,
Brought from the city's torpid laziness
And cleansed in the healing pool. He carries his head   30
Higher now than he did before, and his neck
Is brawnier now. He is proud of the disk on his breast;
He likes his collar; and he likes his belt

[*] Ep. Met. III, 5 (1347) Wilkins tells us that it was a large
white dog of Spanish breed—the royal connections are obscure

127

Made of red cloth, with an embroidery
35 Of snow-white columns. And reminded thus
That you were once his master, he grows proud,
And ready to defy all lesser folk:
The intruding shepherd, pasturing his sheep
Upon my fields, flees with them speedily,
40 And hides them far away. Before my house
He keeps a formidable watch: the villagers
Who once had brought their importunities
Too often to my threshold, come no more,
For fear of him.
45   I live in freedom now,
Since he and he alone is my protector,
And my companion constantly. At night,
When, wearied with the labors of the day,
I seek my couch and close my eyes in sleep,
50 He guards my house; and if I sleep too long
He whimpers, telling me the sun has risen,
And scratches at my door. When I go forth
He greets me joyously, and runs ahead
Toward places often visited, and turns
55 Around from time to time to see if I
Am following; and then, when I recline
Upon the verdant margin of the stream
And there begin again my wonted task,
He starts this way and that, tries all the paths,
60 And then lies down, white on the grassy ground,
Turning his back to me, his face to those
Who may pass by.
              Among the cooling brooks
There is a place where cliff and river meet
65 And only birds are wont to come. I climb
Thereto, with careful steps, and enter in.
He stops, holding the path, with his great body
Blocking the entrance; and if anyone
Should come, he barks to let me know,
70 And then, unless I tell him to be still,
He dashes to defend me. If you note
His ways, you can but recognize in him

Some likeness to our own intelligence.
He leaps to my defense, but if held back
He is quiet: fierce though he be with others   75
He goes in gentleness to meet my friends,
His ears adroop, tail wagging happily.
    Peasants who used to come to me to ask
About the knots of the law, about their rights,
About their households, or a daughter's marriage   80
(As if I were another Appius,
Or an Acilius), and thus disturb
The peace of the Muses, turn away in fear
When he is lying there, across the path.
So now they deal with their own perplexities,
Leaving me to myself, to live my life
As I long to live it: all of this I owe   85
To you, my generous lord.
               Continually
He gives amusement: with great bounds he goes
Through woods and waters; with his shrilly bark
He imitates the children when they sing;
His sudden twists and turns are laughable.   90
He is forever chasing the wild geese:
Over the shore and over the rocks he leaps;
They find no safety even in the stream;
He plunges in, catches them in his mouth,
And brings them out, offering them as a prize,   95
Whether or not one hungers for a feast.
Often he goes a-hunting, and brings back
His booty for my table. Yet for him
All this is play, not wrath—perhaps he likes
To catch the geese as he swims, or does not like   100
Their cackling. He is gentler than a lamb
With weaker creatures. Never would he attack
A sheep, a fleeing she-goat, or a kid.
If a timid hare appear in his way, he stands
As if in fear; yet he would rush upon   105

[81-2] **Appius** probably Appius Claudius Carecus, the Censor;
Acilius M. Acilius Glabrio, tribune, 1st century. Petrarch is
thinking of them as prominent citizens importuned by clients

A breeding sow or a bullock, and would seize
And bite their ears.

                In ancient times, 'tis said
A dog like this was sent to Alexander
As a gift from afar: a beast of royal breed,
110 Scornful of common prey. He would not touch
The creatures of the field, or a fallow deer,
Or bears, or boars, saving his haughty teeth
For nobler wounding. But the hasty tyrant
Thought him a coward, and had him put to death.
115 Another dog was sent him, trained to kill
Fierce lions, and to shake the very ground
Bringing down elephants. Him the youthful prince
Admired, and repented, all too late,
That to the other one he had not offered
Prey worthy of his pride.
120   But I know well
The nature of this dog of mine: a pup
Could bite him with impunity; and yet
He would have no fear of an angry lioness,
Or a tigress reft of her young. You were there, I think,
125 In the papal palace, when there was shown to him
A lion, caged; and with bristling hair he rushed
To break the bars of the cage, and filled the place
With the sound of his furious barking. Taken away
By force, he showed his still unvented wrath
130 In raucous growls and long-continued whining.
    Too much I have written on a theme so slight,
And now have done. But there is one thing more
That I must say. For if there come to us
Folk of your household, whether it be by chance
135 Or on a kindly errand sent—for you
Fail not to hold as present in your thought
Those who are absent, yet are truly yours—
He longs to be within your halls again,
Remembering his former fortune there,
140 And weary of these valleys and these fields.
If he were free to choose, he would return
Again, and rightly, to the lofty Column.

To Italy*

Hail, holiest of countries, dear to God,
Harbour of good men, terror of the proud,
Above all other lands more bountiful,
More fertile and more fair to look upon,
Girt by twin seas, adorned by famous mountains,   5
And venerable for arms and sacred laws,
Home of the muses, rich in gold and men,
On whom both art and nature have bestowed
Rare gifts to make thee mistress of the world!
Long absent now I eagerly return   10
To thee, to stay forever. Thou wilt give
Welcome repose, and when the end has come
Some of thy earth to cover these poor limbs.
Now from the summit of green-leafed Gebenna
On thee I feast my eyes, my Italy,   15
The clouds lie far behind, while a serene
Zephyr caresses me and the mild air
With gentle touch gives me a welcome home.
I know my country and with joy I cry:
Hail fairest mother, glory of the world!   20

* Ep. Met. III, 24; written in 1353   14 **Gebenna** Mt. Genèvre

TRANSLATORS, SOURCES
AND ACKNOWLEDGMENTS

❧

The translators of the Canzoniere are arranged in alphabetical order, according to their first initial as given in the Contents.

AC   Albert Compton (1843-1908): xxxi, ccxc, cccxviii. From *One hundred sonnets of Petrarch,* etc. London, K. Paul, Trench, Trübner & Co., 1898.

BK   Basil Kennet (1674-1715): lxxxi. From *The Sonnets, Triumphs . . . of Petrarch, etc.* London, George Ballard Sons, 1879.

C   James, Earl of Charlemont (1728-1799): cliii. From *Selected Sonnets of Petrarch.* Dublin, W. Folds & Son, 1882.

CBC   C. B. Cayley (1823-1883): v, lxxviii, lxxx, xci, civ, cxlviii, clxxix, ccviii, ccxxxii, cclx, cclxii, cclxix, cccxxxii, ccclxvi. From his *The Sonnets and Stanzas of Petrarch,* London, Longmans, Green and Co., 1879.

CT   Charles Tomlinson (1808-1879): ccx, cccxlvii. From *The Sonnet,* London, J. Murray, 1874.

D   Barbarina Wilmot, Lady Dacre (1768-1854): cxxviii, cccxv. From *Translations from the Italian,* London, C. Whittingham, 1836.

EF   Edward Fitzgerald (1809-1883): xii. From his *Letters and Literary Remains,* London, Macmillan and Co., 1889.

FW   Francis Wrangham (1769-1842): lxi. From *A few sonnets attempted from Petrarch in early life,* Kent, printed at the private press of Lee Priory by J. Warwick, 1817.

GC   Geoffrey Chaucer (1340-1400): cxxxii. First printed by Caxton, ca. 1483.

GFC   Gilbert F. Cunningham (1900-): liii, clxv, cclxiv. Originally written for *Translations from Petrarch,* compiled by T. G. Bergin. Edinburgh, London. Oliver and Boyd, 1955. Reprinted by kind permission of the translator.

JA   Joseph Auslander (1897-   ): lxxxiii, cxx, clxxii, clxxxviii, ccxxi, cclvi, cclxxi, cccxix, cccxxvii, cccxxxvii, cccxlix, From *The Sonnets of Petrarch*, London-New York-Toronto, Longmans, Green and Co. 1931. Reprinted by permission of the publishers.

JAS   John Addington Symonds (1840-1893): xv, cccii, cccxlvi. From *Sketches and Studies in Southern Europe* (Vol. II). New York, Harper and Bros., 1890.

JN   John Nott (1751-1825): clxxxvi, cxcvi, cclxiii, cccxiv. From *Petrarch Translated*, etc. by The translator of Catullus. London, J. Miller, Vernor, Hood, and Sharpe, and S. Bagster, 1808.

JP   John Penn (1760-1834): lxxvii. From *Critical, Political and Dramatic Works*, London, Hatchard, 1796-8.

LH   James Henry Leigh Hunt (1784-1859): cxxvi. From his *Poetical Works* 1860.

MB   Morris Bishop (1893-   ): xvi, xxxii, xxxiii, xxvi, l, lii, lvi, lxii, lxxvi, lxxxvi, xc, c, cii, cxxii, cxxix, cxxxi, cl, clx, cxcix, ccxvii, ccxxii, ccxxiv, ccxxxiv, ccxl, ccxlvi, ccxlviii, ccxlix, ccl, ccliv, cclxvii, cclxxii, cclxxiii, cclxxix, cclxxxi, ccxcii, ccci, cccx, cccxxxvi, cccliii, ccclviii, ccclxv. Originally printed in *Love Rhymes of Petrarch*. Ithaca, the Dragon Press, 1932. Here reproduced by generous permission of the author.

MEW   Maria Eugenia Wrottesley (died 1892): cccxl. From *A Staffordshire Legend, etc*. Wolverhampton, W. Parke, 1851.

RG   Richard Garnett (1835-1906): cxiv, cxxiii, cxlvi, clvi, clxiii, clxviii, clxxiv, clxxx, clxxxv, cxcii, cciv, ccv, ccxi, ccxviii, ccxix, ccxcvi, cccxxi, cccxli. From *cxxiv Sonnets*, London, John Day: Boston, Copeland and Day, 1896.

RGM   R. G. Macgregor (1805-1869): xxii, xxvii, ciii, cxlix, cxcv, ccxxviii. From *Indian Leisure*, London, Smith, Elder and Co., 1854.

S   Surrey, Henry Howard, Earl of — (1517?-1547):

cxl. First printed in *Songs and Sonnettes,* etc., Tottel's Miscellany, London, 1557.

SW — Susan Wollaston (19th century): ci. From *One hundred sonnets after the Italian of Petrarch,* etc. London, E. Bull, 1841.

TCC — Thomas Caldecott Chubb (1899-   ): vii. From *Ships and Lovers,* New York, Albert and Charles Boni, 1933. Reprinted by kind permission of the translator.

TGB — Thomas G. Bergin (1904-   ): i, ii*, iii*, iv, xxx, xxxv*, xl, xli, xlii, xliii, lxviii, lxxiv, lxxxii, xcii, xciii, cxxxiv*, cxlv, clix*, clxiv*, clxxvi*, clxxviii, clxxix, cclix, ccxxviii, cccxi, cccxvi, cclxxiv, cccxxxiii, ccclxiv*. (*Originally appeared in *Lyric Poetry of the Italian Renaissance* edited by L. R. Lind, New Haven, Yale University Press, 1954. Reprinted here by courteous permission of the publisher.)

TW — Thomas Wyatt (1503?-1542): xix was first printed in Tottel's Miscellany, London, 1557. cxxxvi and cxxxviii are attributed to Wyatt by Harington in his *Nugae Antiquae* London, 1769, 1775, but their authorship is uncertain.

TWH — Thomas Wentworth Higginson (1823-1911): clxi. From *Fifteen Sonnets of Petrarch,* Boston, Houghton-Mifflin Co., 1903.

WP — Warburton Pike (1861?-1915): cclxxxvii, cccxii, From *Translations from Dante, Petrarch,* etc. London, C. K. Paul and Co., 1879.

The *Letter to Posterity* is from *Petrarch, the First Modern Scholar and Man of Letters,* by James Harvey Robinson and Henry Winchester Rolfe. New York and London. G. P. Putnam's Sons, the Knickerbocker Press, 1898.

The Metrical Letters I,6 and III,5 are the versions of E. H. Wilkins, reprinted, by permission of the publisher, from his *Petrarch at Vaucluse,* Chicago, University of Chicago Press, 1958. The English of Metrical Letter III,24 is my own.

SELECTED BIBLIOGRAPHY

Two excellent biographies of Petrarch are available in English: the *Life of Petrarch* by Ernest Hatch Wilkins, Chicago, University of Chicago Press, 1962, and *Petrarch and His World* by Morris Bishop, University of Indiana Press, Bloomington, Indiana, 1963. Chapters on Petrarch will also be found in the various histories of Italian Literature now in print, among which may be mentioned those of Francesco DeSanctis (translated by Joan Redfern), New York, Harcourt, Brace & Co., 1931, of E. H. Wilkins, Cambridge, Harvard University Press, 1954, and J. H. Whitfield, Penguin, 1960. T. Mommsen's Introduction to Petrarch's *Sonnets and Songs* translated by Anna Maria Armi, New York, Pantheon, 1946, is valuable. "Petrarch and the Sentiment of Solitude" in S. Quasimodo's *The Poet and the Politician,* S. Illinois University Press, 1964 is brief but acute.

A selection of the letters appears in the volume translated and edited by Robinson and Rolfe (see above under acknowledgments). Mario Cosenza has translated the *Letters to Classical Authors,* Chicago, University of Chicago Press, 1910.

Petrarch's *Secret* has been translated by William H. Draper, London, 1910; a good summary of it may be found in Morris Bishop's biography (*supra.*) E. H. Wilkins has not only translated many of the letters, some metrical, in his *Petrarch at Vaucluse,* but has also given us an English version of the *Triumph,* University of Chicago Press, 1962.

More specialized is *Petrarch, Scipio and the Africa* by Aldo Bernardo, Baltimore, Johns Hopkins Press, 1962.

There have been many editions of the *Canzoniere* since the *editio princeps* of 1470 by Wendelin of Speyer—and of course the poems had circulated in manuscripts for a hundred years before then. Among modern editions that of Ferdinando Neri (Milano-Napoli, Ricciardi, 1951) is highly respected; that of Ezio Chiorboli (Milano, Trevisini, 1924) is rich in commentary.